Opening The Gate

Emily Wiley

To my mom, dad, and twin sister, Katie.

With you I always feel safe.

"There is no normal life that
is free of pain.
It's the very wrestling with our problems
that can be the impetus for our growth."

-Mr. Rogers

Part I

Closing the Gate

June 24th, 2019

One month after "the incident." The evening sun slowly set over the dusky skyline of Hoboken, and the hum of city life buzzed in the air. The honk of cars, the faint hum of music, and the barking of dogs in the distance all floated in the air. I winced at the sound of every bark: a sound that has haunted me in unexplainable ways since the dog attack.

We finally picked a restaurant after twenty minutes of deliberation. Couples and families sat comfortably, soaking in the warm summer bliss and enjoying a glass of wine. As we made our way through the scattered tables on the sidewalk, I latched eyes on our table in the far left corner.

An eagle spotting her prey, I quickly took in the table before me: a rectangle with four chairs and situated next to a wrought-iron gate that kept the tables safely tucked into the restaurant and separate from the street. Now the question was, which seat to sit in. I hesitated, standing frozen in place. I proceeded to test out both sides of the table, near and far. The pro of sitting on the far side, is that I had an ample view of the restaurant around me: it was the captain's chair, with the ability to monitor the fluffy dogs sitting under several tables. But the con was that wrought-iron gate. Glossy gray and rickety, I could tell that the restaurant tried to decorate and refine the gate with a box of purple and pink flowers, but it still could not hide the gap in the gate. A mere twelve inches wide, it may as well have been as wide as the city streets. In my eyes, the gap was a black hole, a dark and intimidating crevice where anything could be sucked in and anything dragged out.

That day in May flooded back to me, and in front of my eyes appeared a similar gate. A creaking, broken gate that connected both sides of the fence around the tennis courts. There was a wide, empty hole stretched across where the two sides of the fence were meant to meet: nearly touching, yet inexorably kept apart. It was only about six inches wide--smaller than the grip of my tennis racket, yet not small enough.

So I chose the near side accordingly, allowing my sharp brown eyes to fix themselves upon the wrought-iron gate to guard myself from everything on the outside. As I stared down at the menu below me, the words and colors started to blend, like water swirling down a drain: penne alla vodka, rigatoni pomodoro. The marble green plastic cover of the table strained my eyes, and a primitive anger filled my chest. The gaudy table cover taunted me, and I felt the urge to rip it from the table and throw it far, far away from me.

My anger melted away into hot, wet tears, the kind that well up in your eyes, waiting for the dam to break and then suddenly rush down your face in a steady stream. Every ounce of emotion I had stifled since the dog attack came rushing back. All I could see was the broken gate, and my mind screamed to shut it.

Now, you might think it odd that I start here. Why tell a gory, climactic story, and start it at an Italian restaurant in the middle of a mental meltdown? Well, that is exactly the essence of this journal itself. The most note-worthy thing about the dog attack is not what happened that sunny day at the park; what's most important is what happened after: the tangle of knots, questions, and fears in my head. I hope that this journal will allow me to untangle these knots and lay out my story. So I can heal.

May 11th, 2019

My family has long discussed that the perfect storm occurred for me to be on that tennis court and for the pit bull to attack me that day. It was my twin sister's tennis lesson so I shouldn't have even been there in the first place, I almost went to fitness instead of tennis, and I could have practiced anywhere else at any other time. We always joke that if my mom had been there with me, she would have thrown her petite five foot one body in front of the dog and protected me-- I know she would have. If it had been any other day, the basketball court next to the tennis courts would have been flooded with players shooting hoops-- people that could have done something when the disaster broke out. Instead, it was virtually only me. That's what confused me: it was the most stunning spring day without a cloud in the sky. It was mild and beautiful weather. Yet there was no one around.

I was taken from the ambulance on a stretcher into the hospital, and I clutched the blood-stained white blankets covering me, my grip turning my hands red and raw. I had finally started to feel the pain that the human body had so expertly fought off when adrenaline had carried me away from danger. I had finished prepping the EMT with my medical history. I remember I warned him, *my family has a history of blood clotting problems: my mom, aunt, and grandmother all do. Will this be a problem?* The EMT laughed but it seemed stiff and forced, and he assured me that everything would be just fine. Looking back, I'm not surprised at all that I asked this; with little else to do other than worry, my type-A personality took over, and I remember my mind exploded with preparations, questions and plans for what was going to happen next. I always have to be prepared.

I had never been to the hospital before-- of course, I had been there once when I was born, but I was a very well-protected and careful child. I had never even broken a bone. My only experience with hospitals were the ones that I admired on television, shows where heroic doctors whisk away patients and succeed in life-saving surgeries that last hours upon hours. They worked briskly and everything was always rapid-paced, go, go, go. This was a stark contrast to the experience I had when I got to the hospital. The biggest thing that I remember was waiting hours upon hours with the clock slowly ticking away. The longer I stared at it, the hands only moved immeasurable amounts.

As time dragged on while I waited for the doctor, pain started to flood my body. I shifted on the hospital bed uncomfortably, thinking that if I put all the pressure on my right leg it would ease the pain. That didn't work, so I tried lying completely on my back. Then I tried sitting upright. But to no avail, the pain lingered and festered. My body shook from trying to balance sitting up, and I flopped back onto the sterile pillows. Darts of pain shot up my leg, and each time I dared to take a peek at the wound, I imagined as though I was being bitten and punctured once again.

I remember my mom's face going pale as she entered the emergency room and saw me for the first time. A rush of relief overcame me to see her warm and comforting face, to know that I was not alone. However, my mom's response was the antithesis to my own: seeing her strong daughter covered in blood as though it had been dumped over her with a bucket did nothing to comfort her. She was clearly concerned. I admired my mom's resolve--or maybe just acting-- as a smile spread across her face, and her voice rose an octave as she chimed "Hi my sweet girl."

She hesitantly stepped through the threshold and thrust herself into the reality of the situation. I watched as she slowly floated over to me, coming in for the inevitable embrace, and she observed my injuries up and down. She winced as she rounded the corner to my right side and peeked below my left leg. I could tell she was trying to be discreet, but with her mouth agape and her fingers trembling, it was obvious she had not expected me to be this broken. I don't think that any mother wants to see the one person they've spent their life protecting so damaged. I was a wounded animal, limping away from her predator and finally in the safety of her mother's arms. I hated feeling this helpless.

My mom went right to work inquiring about a doctor and when I was going to receive help. She did not pry me about what happened, and for this I was fortunate, I was already exhausted and all I wanted was to collapse back onto the hospital bed with it's mediocre pillows and starched blanket: it felt like heaven to me at the time. One of the kind nurses in candy pink scrubs and glasses started to wipe me down with a warm cloth.

"You'll feel a lot better clean," she soothed me, cleaning my arms, legs, chest, and face softly. I was not just bloody, but amazingly dirty, as though I had rolled around in the grass. The nurse rubbed and rubbed, and still a faint red stain remained on my body, an extra layer added onto my tanned skin. The nurse avoided the massive, gaping holes in my body that were exploding with blood, tissue, torn skin--and was that muscle? I wanted to know what was wrong with me. I shot forward, and craned my neck in order to get a closer look at my injuries.

"No, no, no don't worry Emily just relax and lie back," both the kind nurse and my mom ushered me back onto the pillows, struggling to shield me from the extent of my injuries. But it had been too late: I had seen a brilliant, hard white substance sticking out against the deep red wound, and I would later learn that this was my tendon peeking out of my leg. I flopped back against the pillows as the stark hospital lights blinded my eyes and my vision went fuzzy.

My mind was conflicted whether I was amazed or disgusted by the sight of my leg. Part of me found it exciting that I could see the different layers of skin, tendon, and muscle that so intricately make up my body--that allow me to move, run, and play tennis. It was a secret unlocked world and a part of myself I had always been barred from.

A few minutes later, my dad hurried into the hospital, and with a brisk, urgent walk and concerned look, he came to the doorway. He was not as skilled with hiding his emotions as my mom. I noticed his face droop as if someone had pulled the strings down holding up his smile. I nodded as though inviting him in, and his eyes watered with worry.

"Aw Emmy," my dad's voice cracked on the first syllable, and he knelt down next to my bed and started to rub my arms like he always does to comfort me.

"You should have seen her before" my mom laughed uncomfortably, and we gave each other forced and knowing smiles, two people sharing a secret. With my dad cradling me on my left and my mom hugging me from the right, I was enveloped in a warm embrace that almost covered the shivering cold of my pain. Almost.

I vaguely remember hearing snippets of conversation: we had to wait for the plastic surgeon to come, and he was far away and we would have to wait for some time.

I brushed it off saying, "I'm totally fine." I recall reassuring everyone in the room, "I really don't even feel anything."

I remember squeezing my parents' hands, and I felt their energy flowing through our connected arms. It recharged me and wrapped all around me. I felt at ease, conceding that I would at least be able to tell this amazing story. None of my friends would believe it, and I reminded myself that one day this would be a memory. It would be another day in my life that I could look back on and maybe even laugh at. Maybe this was my right of passage into adulthood.

This fleeting relief was short-lived, as the brutal wait slowly melted into physical pain--pain that wracked my whole body and sent sharp knives down my left leg. I was situated in a seated position with my legs splayed out on the bed, and as I readjusted and shifted, a surge went through my body. I began to move constantly as the pain closed in on me and persisted. I groaned and tried to distract myself with conversation, my voice lilting with each searing sensation.

My dad turned on the tv to distract me, and I turned my head to the left to watch from the tiny black screen on the wall. I was simultaneously aghast and amused as the screen lit up to reveal a pride of lions running through the savannah chasing after a lithe antelope. I urged the antelope on *go, go, go* as it struggled against its inevitable fate. The lions sank their teeth into the antelope and relished in their meal. Blood sprayed across the screen. I was the antelope, and I could not watch this. The irony was almost too good to be true.

My parents rushed to change the channel and succeeded in landing on Food network to a new show called Bite Club (I kid you not). I collapsed in a fit of giggles and strong-armed the remote from my parents to turn off the television, which went dark with a click.

"At least you can laugh through this," my Dad chimed in. He plastered a smile across his face, but it was pretty obvious he was struggling--he seemed far more nervous than even myself!

I continued to wait in agony. I tossed and turned to try to position myself comfortably and mask the pain as if I were in a fitful dream. Questions tangled in my mind: how bad is it? Will I be able to go to school Monday? When can I use the bathroom? I filled my head with these simple questions instead of confronting the true gravity of the situation and the larger question looming in the back of my mind: what about the tennis team and my big match on Tuesday?

The last thing I wanted to do at the time was think about what had happened. My brain went into survival mode and shock as my body did, and I put a wedge between my consciousness and that experience. Yet I knew when the policeman knocked on the hospital room door with his stiff uniform and burly build, this safety barrier was ripped from my mind and fell onto the floor. The room became silent.

So I began telling my story: how I had been playing tennis at the Cove Beach park, and a white dog sprinted it's way onto the court and jumped on me with excitement. How when I had finally ushered the dog off the court and shut the gate, the dog fell into a frenzy. How the dog then forced its way through the six-inch-wide gap and charged.

After twenty long minutes and copious concerned questions posed by my parents with very few answers, the policeman left. He shut the door tightly behind him with a resounding finality as it slid into place.

When Dr. Otake arrived, I sensed his surprise as he entered the room, but as an expert plastic surgeon he carefully hid his shock behind a mask of professionalism. I expected him to be serious and stoic; however one of the first things he did was to come right next to me in my hospital bed and shake my hand. It was as though we were headed into a business deal and I was a client he wanted to impress.

The doctor did not rush and immediately begin his work as I had expected him to; instead, he slowly and methodically examined my leg, like an artist observing his work. His face remained placid and unmoving. He was not at all like my parents who had gawked at the immense amount of blood and gore. Rather, Dr. Otake sized up the challenge, and I could see his excited energy radiating from his eyes: he was eager for the adventure ahead.

He walked me through everything that was happening in the surgery as I laid awkwardly on my stomach, shielded from the daunting work he was doing to my leg. I was stabbed with needle after needle and shot after shot to mask the pain, so much so that all I could feel was the tugging and pressure on my skin. Long gone was the searing and shooting pain, and I was left with a cool, numb feeling running down my legs. I had never felt so helpless and out of control, I felt like a torn stuffed animal who was being stitched together again.

Even though I could not see what was happening, I could tell that the surgery was disturbing. My eyes were drawn to my mom's pursed lips and my dad's pale face --he had passed out when my sister and I were born, so I was not surprised.

"It's okay, Daddy, really I'm fine," I reassured him as though he were the child. He had no idea that his discomfort was putting my mind at ease. I was grateful to know I was not the only one struggling.

After hours of pulling and mending my raw skin, over 100 stitches later, it was over. The trauma to my body ended. Lying on my stomach had prevented me from seeing what was happening, but now everything was closed up. I was impressed with the plastic surgeon's magical work, and I felt I was going to be okay.

I'm someone who does not believe in random coincidences; I think that they are often too good to be true, and I like to think that the inner-workings of the earth are deliberate. I like to believe that the complex fabric of our lives are not slapped together haphazardly, and this is something I would struggle with in the coming days, weeks, and even months.

One of these coincidences that day was the two people who were at the hospital and came to see me: one was Mr. Waack, our affable, close family friend who was visiting someone, and the other was my beloved high school tennis coach, Anne-Lise, tending to her own mother. She was the last person I wanted to know that I was injured: I wanted to shield everyone from my high-school team from what had happened and ignore the difficult reality that we would have to face. I had just finished my 13-1 record regular season at number one singles, beating older and more experienced girls who I could now call my rivals. Our team had just finished our stellar season, and the county and state tournaments were at our fingertips.

Yet I felt all of this slipping through my fingers and dissolving just by looking at the irregular array of stitches scattered all over my leg. The dark lines and ties of the stitches repulsed me, and I feared I had become just like the book creature I had read that year in English: I was Frankenstein awakening, a monster. Dark brown patches of bruises began to dot my legs, and fiery red cuts and abrasions seared my legs that had been too small to stitch. I looked broken.

I remember Anne-Lise's soothing voice as she tried to sway my mind away from the tennis team. Tears welled in my eyes and threatened to plunge down my face. My voice cracked each time I spoke. I had barely any energy left to give.

Later that evening, I was pushed out to the parking lot in a wheelchair, and a nurse and I waited in silence as my parents brought the car to the door. The sun was no longer bright and high in the sky, but dusk had settled along with cloudy gray skies, almost knowing that May 11th was no longer a happy day.

"I'm going to be honest," the nurse began cautiously, "Tomorrow will be worse, and maybe the next day and the day after that, but eventually it will get better ." I craned my neck to glance up at her, and she gave me a soft, warm smile. Her words were prophetic, almost like she knew.

As my family helped me hop on my good, right leg to the car and position myself awkwardly in the back seat, my body ached as though I had been punched. I felt like I had been beaten, but the strongest feeling I felt was pure exhaustion. Oh, how I wanted to go home and sink into my bed that was not the sterile, stiff hospital bed that I had called home for seven hours. I was excited to be back outside on this May evening, even if it was only during the short distance from the hospital to the car.

I felt oddly comfortable propped up in the backseat. I felt like a young child again, being driven around. I laughed at the irony of it all: I had gotten my license just two days before. Yet here I was, enjoying the ride in the back of my mom's Toyota. I could not wait to show my sister how bad my injury was--my first real injury! Ha, it was not a chihuahua bite like she had assumed.

Looking back I have no idea why I bubbled with such optimism. At that moment, the only problems and pain I foresaw were missing out on playing tennis with my team. But the fire was stoked in my mind, I was convinced I would be back in time for states.

It was a couple of days later that I learned how lucky I was. If the dog had bit about a centimeter deeper, he would have hit my femoral artery: the main artery that brings blood to your leg. My doctor explained how if the dog had broken through this artery, the whole ordeal would have been even more dramatic, and we would have had a very different conversation.

About a centimeter. I shuddered to think about the power that such a small, seemingly insignificant distance held. It was possibly life and death.

At first, I was amazed by how many things went wrong that day to concoct this perfect storm of a disaster. But then I started to consider everything that went right--everything that fell into place to protect me. What if the dog had gone for my face? What if when I fell to the ground, I hadn't fought my way back up? What if I had curled up in a ball and just waited for the predator to finish off its prey? So many "what ifs" swam in my mind, that I began to feel lucky. Like some invisible hand was protecting me from a far worse fate. I had survived, and any time I felt depressed and cheated, I would remember that.

After coming home from the hospital, I fell asleep that night at 9:30: unheard of for a teenager on a Saturday night. As I collapsed onto the soft pillows of my bed, my mom promised me: "Sleep. You'll feel better tomorrow."

These were the same words she uttered to me years before when I got my first palate expander to fix my teeth. I remember the straining, uncomfortable pain in my mouth and every time I tried to breathe I felt restricted. I tried to harness the strength that I had when I was just nine years old, and I felt a sense of reassurance.

May 12th, 2019

When I woke up the next morning, the events of the day before blurred in a haze--it all seemed far-fetched to me. The bits and pieces of my memory wove together, and I was amazed by what had happened. It was almost comical that I had been brutally attacked by a dog the day before--I mean, who does that happen to?

When I first described what happened to my sister the morning after the incident, her eyes grew large. I had never seen her so intently focused, quiet, and in utter awe.

"Wow. I thought that you just got one teeny bite from a yappy dog and made a whole fuss about it," my twin sister, Katie, confessed, shaking her head.

I don't think anyone was prepared for the severity of this accident: not my parents when they were blindsided walking in the hospital doors, not my teammates who were excited about FCIAC's starting next week, and not my friends who were devastated for me. No one expected happy-go-lucky Emily to have such an encounter.

I think part of the reason why I was so optimistic throughout my whole recovery was I was a little naive. The first days of my injury were long and painful, but I trudged forward with the vision that I would be back and healed for the state tournament. I don't know if it was the cliché sports comeback story or my own unwavering ambition that created these goals for myself, but these unrealistic dreams carried me through this difficult period.

The first day I was weaker than ever before. Bed-ridden, I could not hold myself up and my leg pulsed with pain. It was unimaginable pain, worse than I had ever experienced, but something in me knew that I could handle it. I think that's why I pasted on a smile and stated proudly, "It hurts, but I can manage. I'm going to be okay." Almost immediately, that fake smile faded into a real one.

I never once talked back to my parents or complained that I was in too much pain, and I only groaned "why me" for about ten minutes. I was smacked in the face with a realization: there was no rhyme or reason why this happened to me or why unfortunate things happen to anyone.

As my body weakened, I felt my mental resolve harden, like how when a person loses their sight, their sense of hearing heightens to compensate. I resisted needing help to do simple tasks, and I felt guilty relying on my family for basic needs such as fetching me water.

That first day after the incident was Mother's Day, and I had never appreciated my mom more than that day. Normally, she would drag us all to her favorite pizza restaurant where we would celebrate, but I had foiled the one day of the year set aside just for her. That Mother's Day, I remember feeling so gross and dirty from the hospital the night before. I desperately needed a shower. But the shower posed a problem, because I could not stand. I could not make it over the ledge into the shower, I could not reach the shampoo or soap, and I could not maneuver myself or put any pressure on my left leg.

Needing help to bathe was one of the most defeating experiences I felt during the first week of healing. I felt horribly that I had added a burden to our daily routines. I remember my mom holding my shoulders and helping me into the shower. She helped me balance as I cleaned myself: I felt like a baby. But, it also came into focus how much I still needed my mom and how she would sacrifice her day to help me, even though I had stolen her thunder. So on Mother's Day, my mom lovingly helped me to shower, reminding me of everything that she had done for me since I was born and everything she would willingly do forever on.

May 13th, 2019

This was the only day that I missed school. The Blue Wave Girls Tennis team was in the running for the Ruden Report Team of the Week. My team. I felt on the outskirts of everything, behind an invisible glass looking in on something that had once felt so familiar. I felt so helpless slumped on the brown leather chair in our family room, trapped inside of my house and my injury.

We had just closed our successful regular season: just that week we had won all three of our matches and finished senior day with a bang. My personal season at number one singles--the position I had only dreamed of playing and I had trained for for years-- slammed to a close. With wins against older girls, including the eventual 2019 state champion, I felt that my success had been ripped out of my hands. It left me with an emptiness that only tennis could fill.

My personal agony could not compare to the guilt and pain I felt for my team. For a team that had endured every possible stroke of bad luck—including two disqualifications from state championships the years before-- I felt I had let everyone down. My coaches, team, and family reassured me that there was nothing I should feel guilty for: fate is the force that dealt us all such a poor card.

With my absence, the whole line-up shifted and we were going to be catapulted into the FCIAC team tournament unsteady and unstable, missing a peg. That's the difficult thing about high school tennis: even though it is a notoriously individual sport, losing any member of the team is like a cannon-hole in a ship, causing it to slowly sink.

When I heard that we were nominated for the Ruden Report team of the week, I craved this small victory like no other. The Ruden Report is a popular local website that covers our county's high school sports. Every week, several sports teams are nominated for outstanding performance, and individuals vote for coveted bragging rights. Although incapacitated and feeling more pain that my body had desperately shielded me from before, I knew we had to win this glorious team of the week prize.

I texted everyone in my contacts: family members, cousins, friends from school, friends from tennis. I voted using every email I had. Up against six other local sports teams, somehow we won, and I like to think that karma had my back on this one. We won a t-shirt, but at that moment in time, it felt like everything.

May 14th, 2019

My first day back at school. First days of school are typically exciting milestones, filled with meeting new teachers and finding out who is in each of your classes. I am a rare breed of individuals that loves school: learning, seeing my friends everyday, and most importantly playing on the tennis team. This first day back to school was entirely new in its own way. I wasn't nearly as excited.

Everyone always assumes that as a result of the injuries I sustained, I must have missed weeks of school. They would be surprised to learn that this was not the case at all: I only missed one day of school. I begrudgingly missed it too, as I always try to be in class and have a compulsive fear of missing information and getting behind--ahh the stressors of high school.

My parents and I had tried to arrange with the school a way for me to Skype into my classes--at least for the first week--as I continued to heal. My motion was still very limited, and I was in pain. But to no avail, for privacy reasons we couldn't arrange this for some of my classes. So, three days after the attack, I rallied, and I was back at school.

Darien High School is unique in how spread out it is. The school campus is shaped like a circle, and it had never felt larger and more daunting than when I was on crutches. I had assumed it would be fun: I had never been on crutches before and I got to leave class a few minutes early and take the elevator.

How I appreciated taking the stairs after this experience. I gained a newfound appreciation for being able to walk and control my body, even if it meant walking all the way across the courtyard or trudging my way to third floor French.

After propelling myself down the hallway a couple yards, I would lean against my crutches for a break, exhausted. *Man, I thought, how can I already be out of shape? It's only been 3 days without tennis.* Maneuvering around school was simply exhausting, and my body was already drained from the healing process. Every ounce of my body was focusing its energy on healing my leg, and I felt like the rest of me had shut down.

I was panting and sweating, but I urged myself forward in fear of the bell. That was the one sound I did not want to hear, but that first day of school I had failed: the hallways swarmed with students piling out of their classes like a tsunami wave. The relentless fast-walkers shoved their way around me, and I felt myself being pushed and prodded. I clung to the wall and just waited for it all to stop, to be able to float to the surface of the ocean of people.

In essence, that was my first day back at school. But I also faced another problem: I would have to tell people what happened. That day back at school I was a magnet, with my leg swaddled in a wrap and leaning on crutches. My presence attracted the attention of every room I entered. I wasn't sure if I liked it or not.

It was exhausting, yet oddly comforting telling my story over and over again. Each time I told the story, I felt as if I remembered a new detail, like I was piecing together the fabric of an incredibly complex quilt.

But after telling my story for the seventh time--one for each period of the day-- I had whittled down my classmates' reactions to one of two responses: the "I am so sorry that must have been horrible. Feel better," and the "Woah, that's sick, you're gonna have some wicked scars."

I had expected people to be in utter shock and bewilderment, as my family and close friends had been--this was not something that happens every day. But it was surprising--and relieving--to hear every now and then that a friend of a friend had gone through something like I had. Interestingly enough, my math teacher had been bit by a dog when he was young. Most of the stories I heard were of small bites, but it felt comforting to know that I was not an anomaly and that I was not suffering alone.

That day had been draining physically and emotionally. When the last bell of the day rang at 2:20, I trudged my way to the car on my crutches. Then I came right home and fell fast asleep on the couch.

May 15th, 2019

I emerged from the warm cocoon of my home and out into the spring air. I heaved myself through the French doors leading to the backyard, my right arm clinging to the door and my left arm wrapped around one of my crutches. I cautiously dipped down the lone stair to the stone porch floor. It was the tallest single step I had ever known. My mom furrowed her brow with worry behind me and supported my back as I hopped one-legged to the couch. I balanced myself expertly on my strong right leg, honing my 5th grade gymnastics experience.

I felt the right calf muscle pulsing, contracting, and growing stronger and stronger with each step that I took. Meanwhile, my weak left leg paled in comparison; I could almost feel the years of carefully toned tennis muscles dissolving with every minute that passed.

I could tell my mom winced with each hop I took, even though my back was turned away from her.

"I'm fine, Momma. I'm still in shape," I reassured my mom, the limitless optimism rushing over my body that is the product of innocence. I still believed I would be back and ready to play in the state championships.

Yet even I knew that as I made the fifth and final hop to the couch, I was exasperated. I collapsed backwards in relief, feeling the strong soothing arms of the couch embrace me.

Lying back on the couch and closing my eyes was pure bliss. When I closed my eyes it felt for a second as if the whole world had disappeared except for myself, and there was only me, my steady breathing, and my consciousness. And the sound of dogs. I had never noticed before how simply sitting silent in the spring, the sound of dogs barking flooded my mind. I could hear the echoing sound from far away, and I could tell my heart beat faster every time. If I blinked I was back at the tennis courts at the Cove, adrenaline rushing through my veins. I could hear the dog barking wildly after the tennis ball, then later as it growled and tore through my skin.

When I wasn't in school, I spent the better part of the spring cradled by the white wicker couch with the blue and white striped cushions on my back porch. Every crisp morning and humid afternoon I passed on this couch. My couch. My sanctuary. It was not just the couch that provided me comfort, but the lush foliage of the neighboring

Woodland Park trees, the peaceful bird songs that lilted through the air, and the wide picket white fence that ran along the edge of my backyard, hugging me in and keeping me safe.

Every time I sat on the back porch, I had grown into a habit. I sat up each time, craned my neck, and looked left and right. The gates were shut and locked. Good. The gate was my security blanket, and every time I heard a dog bark in the distance I would take a peek to make sure everything was shut. I knew that each time I glanced at the gate I was caving into my fear. But I craved the feeling of safety that the secure, latched gate provided, and I believed that nothing could push its way into my little oasis. The beautiful white fence guarded me, and was the only separation from my backyard and the woods.

I had never realized the sheer amount of dogs that would pass by my house on a daily basis. I live next to a nature preserve, and this forced me to confront my trauma: the woods was a free-for-all for dogs. A dog heaven. I suddenly seemed to notice every time that a playful dog would bark in the distance or when an owner would take a stroll with his or her dog in the park. It was almost like I had a radar for them--a heightened sense for when dogs were near. The hairs would rise on my back, and I could feel goosebumps dotting my arms and legs.

The first time that this happened was my first day sitting outside again. A stunning, cool May day without a cloud in the sky, much like the one on the tennis courts just four days earlier. I had just settled onto the couch when I heard the roar of a dog in my ears. I hopped from the couch with a rush of energy and sprung on my right leg, and in two giant leaps, I was back in the house. I slammed the French doors shut behind me and slid to the floor. My dad peered around the corner, surprised to see me back inside and confused how I managed to get there.

It was ironic that one of the first days I was home after the dog attack, my next door neighbor brought home a brand new dog for her kids. It was just a puppy, with a silky reddish-brown coat and small waddly legs. Yet I remember shaking in fear knowing that for the first time there would be a dog next door: a constant reminder that I could never escape from my fear. Looking back now, it's hard to believe that I was intimidated by such an innocent creature, but back then I was always on edge for something to come up and attack me from behind. I had always thought that my backyard was my haven, where I could be safe and shielded from the world. I didn't feel safe going for walks anymore. I didn't feel safe going over to my friends' houses for the longest time. I never even went in the woods anymore, where I had just taken a leisurely walk the day before the incident.

I knew that I should not feel this way about the fluffy, innocent creatures that I had once begged my parents for. But, the dog that attacked me was not innocent: it had been out for blood. I could still distinctly hear his low growl, punctuated by the tearing as he latched onto me. It sounded hungry and evil, yet it didn't bark at me. This is the contradiction that I grappled with, because this dog was all bite, and no bark.

May 16th 2019

The calm before the storm had subsided. The severity of my injury had finally begun to rear its ugly head, both visually and painfully. As I continued to heal, the internal damage that the dog attack had caused began to manifest itself on my skin for the world to see. I had thus far carried the mentality that *it could have been worse,* believing that my leg had healed very cleanly. However, new marks began to reveal themselves and made me feel less secure with my progress. Heavy bruising covered my left leg haphazardly, giving me the appearance of someone beaten up in a fight. Stark, black stitches that looked as if they had sewn a broken doll back together dotted my legs. Still, I uttered *it could have been worse.*

To tell the truth, I did believe that everything could have been worse. Fate had dealt me an unlucky hand, but I fought against the notion that I was an "unlucky" person. Yes, I was attacked by a dog while playing tennis a few days earlier. Yes, I had encountered several other unfortunate situations like having a cyst in my mouth take out a permanent tooth, and I concussed myself by hitting my head on a giant palapa umbrella, but other than that I believed that I was a blessed person.

Yet even lucky people are not immune to pain. I had faced the sharp pains at the hospital and the perpetual stabbing of needles pushing more numbing medicine into my body. The pain followed me home and manifested itself into a dull, throbbing that persisted each day and night. The worst was when I tried to put any pressure on my left leg, or if I bent it awkwardly. It felt like my leg was being compressed under massive weight, and aching pains would shoot up and down my leg.

As I rolled out of bed each morning after the attack, I was not surprised to see the tennis-ball sized swelling gathering around my ankle and bulging from my wound--the doctor had stressed that this was the natural healing process. So, I went about each day casually, fading into my new normal: I was oddly happy, and I could cover up my wound with a pair of leggings or a leg wrap. But as time wore on, my mood changed as did the appearance of my left leg.

The "healing process" that the doctor had described felt entirely counter-intuitive. The coloring of my leg morphed from the deep tan that I had gained from the tennis season, to a tepid yellowish-green and brown color that extended haphazardly all along my lower left leg. I noticed my skin continuing to re-generate and tighten around the stitches, leaving a clear orange pus behind. It started to seep out of the stitches and leave my legs with an oily sheen. My leg continued to swell and bulge, larger than my right leg. It was a sickening and unnatural sight, far from what I envisioned to be "healing." I was simultaneously fascinated and ashamed by it.

I fought back tears before a dam broke and they would never be able to stop flowing. My optimism wavered, but as I watched my parents and sister's sad and pitying smiles, I snapped myself back into focus. Something had changed in me over these past couple of days. I had always loved to be nurtured and taken care of, and I loved the feeling of being taken under my mother's wing. But the hidden concern and saddened eyes that screamed pity is what irritated me the most--more than concentrating in class when my leg flared up in pain. More than the annoyance of showering that was an hour-long ordeal. More than watching a match behind a glass wall as my tennis team moved on without me. More than anything, I did not want to be the subject of anyone's pity.

I think that's why I made light of what happened most of the time. I joked about being attacked by the dog, and I noticed the ironies whenever I could. But I often blocked out the real sadness and trauma I felt and how upset I truly was by what happened to me. I still harbored a deep-seeded fear inside of me: a fear of dogs and the feeling that I was never truly safe. By pushing something I deemed silly down, I buried my anger. It was only a matter of time before my foundation began to crumble.

May 17th, 2019

One day that will live in infamy was a certain drive home from school when I was still subjected to crutches. In order to get to my house after leaving the high school, we have to pass the middle school traffic, which gets out of school at about the same time as I do. The line is dizzyingly long, and the road is often a parking lot. It is the worst possible thing I can endure after a long day of school propelling myself down hallways on my crutches. It is excruciatingly slow.

I practically ripped the steering wheel into my own hands in order to make the turn onto a side street and cut around the traffic.

"Oh, just let me drive!" I joked, as we finally sped away onto the empty street.

"Sure, if you want," my dad replied nonchalantly, slowing the car to a stop and unbuckling his seat belt.

"What?" I asked, confused. My dad had finally bought the new car he had been waiting for for years, and I had only gotten my license two weeks before. Even worse, I was unable to move my left leg and still relied on crutches. It was one of those bizarre things that my dad sometimes suggested, and I was not going to miss this opportunity.

My dad opened the back door to grab my crutches, but I shook my head voraciously, instead hopping on my right foot all the way around to the driver's seat thinking, *I'm a licensed driver, I don't need help getting into a car. I can drive!*

As I slipped into the new leather seats and behind the wheel, I felt power surge in my hands, the roar of the engine, and the thrill of freedom. It was that same feeling I had felt two weeks earlier when I had finally gotten my license. I remember conquering that rite of passage, and flying down the street that morning of the incident. I rolled the windows down to let the wind flip through my hair, and I turned up the music slightly louder than my mom preferred. I hadn't been in the driver's seat since.

With a deep breath, I flashed an excited smile to my dad. I pressed my right foot on the brake, letting my left leg hang loosely on the side, useless. I pulled the car into drive and felt it lurch forward which made me catch my breath. As we rolled away down the side road, the sheer mechanical power of a car flowing through my veins, all I could think was: *don't crash this very new car.*

May 18th, 2019

I was continually amazed by how much love I had received from the accident; I was astonished by how much people cared and were hurt by this. Beautiful pastel flowers encircled the outdoor couch. I didn't think that I had ever received flowers before; their lush beauty soothed me. Family friends brought an abundance of delicious food, from cookies to fruit bouquets to entire meals. Food truly is one of my weaknesses.

Candy from my friends piled high on the table, and their visits brought joy to my otherwise brutal days. When some of my friends first came to see me, I could feel their concern radiating off of them, and they hesitantly entered the room, not sure what they were going to find. I'm someone who needs contact with other people, and it was hard at first not being able to relish in the late-spring weather with my friends. But just seeing them for little bits of time re-energized me like a battery. I had never realized how many people cared about me.

I also received cute get-well cards that brought a glimmer to my eye. My tennis teammates made me a gigantic card out of a purple and blue poster board that everyone signed and adorned with the kindest words. I had never had this much love spilled for me, and I still have that giant card to this day.

May 19th, 2019

One of the most difficult experiences that came from the attack was having to re-learn how to walk. It's something that I never thought about before and that I used to take for granted.

It was strange not being able to fully control my left leg because my lower calf was numb. If you had tickled my calf or even hit it, I would have had no idea. It bothered me at first. I was so anxious touching and rubbing my leg, but I couldn't feel any sensation at all, as if I wasn't even touching it. It was almost the absence of pain that bothered me more than the searing pain itself. It scared me to think about how long it would be before I could feel anything there, and I craved to feel something, to reassure that I was alive.

In the early days, when I was gripped with concern and longed for the nerves in my leg to work, I would grab onto my good right leg. I would scratch and pinch and slap my leg in order to remind myself that my body wasn't completely broken. I would scratch so hard that I would leave scrape marks along my legs, white abrasions that would turn red. My skin was so fragile, but the pain felt good. It reminded me that I could feel.

The doctor had told me that nerves regenerate slowly, and it would be months if not years before the nerves would heal and my leg could fully feel again. What scared me is that this would take longer than the actual wounds to heal: there was damage underneath that I could not even see. Damage that would take time to fix.

I'm getting off topic, but to return to walking, I relished in the stability of the crutches, and the white wicker couch on the back porch had become my home base. I found warmth and strength on that couch--I would lie down on it, and I felt at ease. I had only been on crutches for one week when I noticed that the muscles in my left leg were stiffening. My right leg was strengthened and toned from carrying the weight of my whole body, whereas my left leg shrunk in comparison--apart from the swelling--and remained weak and immobile. My bad leg was completely worthless.

My dad jarred me awake when he instructed me:

"You need to start walking. You have to do it or it will be an uphill battle from here."

His sharp words brought my reality into focus. The crutches were giving me fiery red abrasions on my underarms as I leaned on them for support. My left leg was bent at a near right angle when I was most comfortable, and every time that I tried to straighten it, my leg rebelled. My ankle was continually swelling from lack of circulation and the fluid from my injury settled down there. The scar tissue near the back of my knee was hardening, and it was only a matter of time before it reached a point of no return. I had to start walking again.

My mom and dad would hold each of my arms, bearing much of my weight, but even putting the slightest bit of pressure sent excruciating pain radiating up and down my left leg.

I was annoyed at my dad's firm tone and encouragement for me to walk: I felt I needed more time to heal, and my body was still exhausted from the trauma. I didn't think that I could do it; I felt like an ant-sized creature staring at the base of a daunting mountain. Yet after hopping dependently on my right leg, playing a game of "the floor is lava" tiptoeing from couch to couch, chair to chair, and sliding on my backside down the stairs, I was ready.

The first time I *really* walked, I was alone. I was lying outside on the back porch, as per usual, and I had had enough. I was wracked with anger and the ambition to walk. I knew if there would ever be the slightest possibility that I could join my team and play tennis again this season, I had to walk. Even more than that, I could not bear the helplessness I felt as a prisoner to the couch: I felt betrayed by my body that had always been so strong.

I jumped into the abyss head first. I almost didn't even think about it. Suddenly, I had sprung off the couch and tiptoed my way across the grass and onto the paved stones surrounding the pool. I walked like I had forgotten that anything had changed: there was no before and after the accident, just the now. I screamed with delight,

"Momma, look! Come now!" I begged her to take a video of me to capture this moment, her baby's first steps. She indulged me as I tiptoed triumphantly around the pool, radiated with a renewed sense of energy. She was the one who had to tell me to slow down and take my time before I re-injured myself.

I didn't know back then about the exaggerated limp and leaning gait I had in my walk. I didn't know back then how slowly I was walking, like a stumbling baby bird attempting to take flight. Back then, I vainly believed that because I was walking, I would be healed in time to join my team and play in states. It's hard to pinpoint exactly why I was so optimistic during my entire injury and physical recovery, but I think I have these youthful fantasies to thank.

May 20th, 2019

It was difficult to juggle my relief and joy at my improvement physically and my own despair at watching what felt like the world go on without me. Although I had made great strides in taking my first steps, these sudden bursts of energy were not enough to propel me back to normal for the time.

Crutches would still remain a staple in my life for a while. This switch that I envisioned I would flip that allowed life to go back to normal was non-existent.

I watched as a spectator from the sidelines for my team's first match of the FCIAC tournament--the first match without me. The black chain link fence in front of me obstructed my eyes from clearly seeing the matches, and it became an impenetrable barrier. I was on the other side of my team, looking in. I felt like I was looking in on myself and my past like a hologram, and I saw the many formative moments that occurred on these exact same courts. I saw myself as a twelve year old playing at summer camp. I saw myself practicing with my friend anxiously in the cold before our first tryouts freshman year. I saw my biggest wins on these courts, and I saw myself staring back at me with that glimmer in her eyes and biting her lip in concentration.

These happier times meshed with the reality that I was still sitting in my folding chair with my leg propped up and swaddled in a blanket: nothing more than a spectator. I felt pitying stares soak into my skin, and I had the sudden urge to rise up out of my chair and walk around--to feign normalcy, because I did not want their pity.

I decided to fake my happiness until suddenly I realized my smiles came instinctively. I still ate bagels ravenously with my team as I had always done before. I cheered wildly for my team, leaving my voice raw and empty. These traditions reminded me that I was still here--the same Emily, doing anything she could for her team.

With a sudden burst of energy, I pushed myself out of my chair and neglected my crutches. I limped along the sides of the court, pacing to show off my incredible prowess for walking. I wanted people, especially the other team, to notice that I could come back soon, that I was still just as much of a threat as I was before. I hoped that people would feel intimidated by me and my "quick" recovery. I'm not sure if anyone else took these power moves seriously, but I vainly believed that I would be back in time for states for that cliché sports injury, come-from-behind victory. I'll let you know that these fantasies fell through. Instead, I needed to sit back down because my leg was cramping.

May 21st, 2019

The next natural step in any recovery process is physical therapy. So that's what I did. Ten days after the accident, my mom brought me to see Mike Morgan, an expert physical therapist whom my family has sworn by for years and we claim can work miracles. We go to Mike for all of our sports injuries-- my Dad as a golf professional and my sister, mom, and myself as avid tennis players. In fact, I had just seen Mike Morgan a couple of weeks prior, and he had healed my knee with little effort. I think this is why Mike was so shocked to have me come in for this completely new and unconventional issue. But I believed in him nonetheless.

I stumbled into Mike's office, still relying heavily on my crutches. The Frankenstein stitches dotted the back of my knee and the majority of my calf, coupled with grotesque bruising and swelling, not to mention the fact that I hadn't shaved this area of my leg for well over a week.

After I had hoisted myself up onto the patient's table and settled down, Mike looked at my leg in awe. For a few minutes, he stayed silent, taking everything in. I didn't know whether he was disgusted, confused, uncertain or all three. But he got to work anyways as if this were just another one of my tennis injuries.

My motion was still very limited at this point, so we started off that first day with Mike just massaging my leg. I had never known a massage to hurt before, but this one sure did me in. My wound was still so tender and sore, and I had been reluctant to touch this area of my leg, let alone press down hard on it. I winced in pain and shut my eyes, burying my head in my arms like I was pretending to take a nap. But my kicking and reflexes gave me away.

Mike reassured me calmly that he knew this was a hard and painful process, but we needed to start therapy. We had to start working before the scar tissue set in-- the stiff tissue that builds up around an injury as it tries to repair itself. We had to get me back in motion as soon as possible before the permanent damage set in, stiffening my leg and preventing me from moving.

Stumbling out of the office on my crutches after our hour was up, I felt aches and pains all over. It was funny how lying on a patient's table drained the little energy I had left these days. My mom always commented on how exhausted I was during my recovery. My body was like a war zone. The sergeant sent out all its troops in my body to focus on healing the traumatized area behind my knee where the injuries were concentrated. The soldiers marched systematically in a line to the war zone, sustaining dark purple and yellow bruises during the battle. Meanwhile, energy supplies ran low and were used up faster and faster as the ammunition was fired at the deep wounds on my calf.

While the wounds were stitched together, there were some casualties in the process. The minor scrapes on my right leg that were left without stitches are neglected to this day. The dark brown lines and discoloration from the dog's claws are etched across my upper thigh and still stand as persistent reminders of the battle. Although the skin on my left leg was bound together, the bumpy purple mountains remained behind, vestigial features of that day on the tennis courts.

While the soldiers held down the fort in my body, the enemy charged the other, vulnerable bank: my mind. This psychological battle was not a structured, traditional fight, but guerilla warfare that would attack suddenly, then fade out of view until I felt like I was safe. Feeling safe and being safe: I began to see no difference.

One time I was snuck up on was that day coming home from physical therapy. My mom saw it before I did, and I noticed her face grow pale and wan. She brought the car to a halt, conflicted with what to do next. Confused, I asked her:

"What? What's wrong, what are you looking at?" Then I saw it. I was in utter shock that I couldn't even let out the gasp that was waiting on my lips. In front of our car on the way home from my first day of physical therapy was a white pit bull, walking down our little, dead-end street. It was identical to the dog that attacked me with the same silky white coat and piercing, black eyes. He fought against his owner and his leash and continued to walk nonchalantly in the direction of the woods, towards my house.

At that moment I was transported back to the tennis courts at the Cove. I was staring into the dark eyes of the dog as it wiggled it's way through the gate, then charged at me. I blinked and I was in the car again, watching the dog lope down our street towards my safe haven. Our car cautiously edged forward. I wanted to feel safe and let it not bother me. Instead, I squeezed my mom's hand. I waved my white flag.

May 25th, 2019

A couple of days later, I was scheduled for my first follow-up appointment with Dr. Otake. My heart beat in my chest as the elevator lifted my family and me to his upstairs office. Normally, only one of my parents accompany me to my doctor's appointments. I could tell this one was different.

"He's going to be so impressed with your improvement. That's my girl, bouncing back tougher than ever," my dad squeezed my shoulders in that motivational way that he always does. He seemed proud, and I wondered what I had done. I could barely even walk yet.

When we entered the sleek, modern office I got this uncomfortable feeling in the pit of my stomach. I looked around the waiting room and saw people sitting comfortably on the white couches. But what bothered me was there did not seem to be anything obviously wrong with these patients. My eyes wandered to the walls lined with pamphlets for botox and other cosmetic surgeries. Suddenly, my mind was flooded with worries: what if I have scars that never heal? What if I always walk with a limp? What if my leg will always have that indent from the pulling of the stitches?

All things considered, I had always felt like my legs were healing wonderfully. But suddenly, I felt ashamed by the cloth wrap falling down my left leg. I re-fastened my wrap and tried to hide my crutches the best that I could. But it was all in vain, because even in doing this, I could not hide the red abrasions and scrapes that still lined my right leg and the bruises that decorated my knees.

When we were called into Dr. Otake's office, I picked up my crutches and limped to the door. Each movement of the crutches sent a thundering echo across the room. I felt eyes watching me, looking me up and down and wondering what had happened to me. As I entered his office, I sank into the patient's chair with relief.

His office was a drastically different sight from the emergency room that I had last seen him in. I took in everything before me: sleek tile floors, granite countertops and a leather patient's seat. Dr. Otake's office was an oasis. Instinctively, I carefully crossed my good right leg over my wounded left leg, vainly attempting to hide the chaotic stitches and ghastly colors underneath. I felt that my bum leg was ruining the perfect environment.

I worried about what Dr. Otake would think - - were the deep cuts healing fast enough? Was this color natural? Should it feel this sore? A student trying to please her teacher, I craved good marks on this first examination after surgery.

I watched my parents sit cautiously down into two of the chairs in the room. My mom expertly pulled out her legal pad and began taking notes. My dad furrowed his brow, and I could already tell that questions were forming on his lips. The concerned parent look comes naturally to them.

Dr. Otake came into the room and proceeded to shake my hand just like he did the first time I saw him. Politely, he asked if he could remove the wrap and take a look at my leg. Of course I said yes, because what other choice did I have?

I cringed as my crippled leg was exposed in all of its glory. My parents and I scanned Dr. Otake's face for any sign of emotion, any indication of how my recovery was going. Keeping a straight and objective face, he turned to me and told me that I looked fantastic, and my body was doing a great job of healing.

After addressing me, he looked joyfully at my parents, who subsequently relaxed their shoulders and sighed with relief. My dad's brow unfurrowed and my mom sunk back into her chair after perching on the edge like a hawk. Dr. Otake then began outlining our plan and some things I would do in the future to help heal my leg: use scar tape, apply bright white zinc sunscreen, etc. But what I was most taken by was how the whole time Dr. Otake looked me in the eyes and gave me the game plan. I was used to doctors treating me like a child or a science experiment and giving my parents the run-down on *my* health like I was not even there. I loved how he spoke to me, the patient.

Leaving the office that day, all I wanted to do was show off my improving walking skills. I strutted down the hallway of the doctor's office, the receptionists cheering me on. In reality, I limped unsteadily for a couple of feet, but I might as well have been walking down a runway.

"I'm so proud of my body" I giggled.

June 20th, 2019

As the days faded in and out, each summer day like the last, I felt like I was losing part of myself. It was one of these days that I ran horrified to my mom with a realization--a realization that chewed up my soul and spit it out. My callus was fading away.

This may seem like a silly thing to most, but to me, it felt as if I had lost a relative, lost a layer of myself or a protective guardian. That rough, raised callus just below my pinky on my right hand has been in my life since I started playing competitive tennis--since I was around nine years old. Over seven years I've had this rough, mountainous bump.

Flipping over my palm, my callus is lighter compared to the rest of my hand--almost yellow--and is etched with deep, white lines. Cringe-inducing to some, my callus never hurts me and somehow always feels like home. In my callus are the long hours on the tennis court roasting in the hot summer, the frustration I felt after changing my forehand for the seventh time, and the victory of a straight-set win against an opponent I once lost to. Sometimes I'll trace my callus nonchalantly with my left hand, absent-mindedly transporting me back to the days when I was not afraid to step onto a tennis court--when I could play tennis in the first place.

As my hands timidly touched the jagged, ghastly scars that formed on my left leg, I craved the smooth sensation of baby soft skin that doesn't have to hide from the sun. But in my hands hide the truth: my skin has never been that way. My legs may be rough, but so are my hands. They are not the feminine hands that many aspire to have: they're the rough, firm hands of a worker, of someone who spends hours each day honing her craft. They're the hands of a tennis player, and that's just the way I like it.

As I noticed my callus slowly begin to soften and the bump become less and less pronounced, I felt my foothold on the tennis world weaken. I felt the sport that had been my lifeline slip between my fingers.

This shock jarred me, and I lamented to my mom how I felt I was losing myself. I had always been the tennis player, and sitting in the shade that summer instead of out on the courts training felt like a failure. Losing this facet of myself made it hard to breathe, and I gasped for air but nothing would come out. I breathed heavier and heavier, but it felt like I was trying to breathe underwater in vain. No air seemed to fill my lungs and my chest heaved up and down. I thought it was my allergies, but I knew this asphyxiation was not nature's fault: it was fate rearing its ugly head.

Searching for air, I needed to ground myself in something. I eased myself into the grass, and sat staring up at the rich blue sky. The canopy of trees nestled around my house like a cocoon and held me close. The soft wind gave birth to goosebumps on my arms and rustled the bushes. The sweet fragrance of hydrangeas tickled my nose. The dewy grass between my toes connected me to the muddy earth; I felt energy surge through my body, and I breathed.

That's the first time I meditated and I didn't even know it yet. In my chaotic world of sports practices, homework, and competition --a world we all live in to some extent--I adore these ten minute meditations that have become my routine. Meditation grounds me and relaxes me. Sometimes

I'm sitting outside on my favorite back-porch spot. Other times I'm nestled on the small, fluffy carpet in my room, or maybe I'm scratching away in my notebook, lost in a sea of consciousness and a steady flow from mind to paper. Meditation has healed me. Maybe this book is a meditation of its own.

June 25th, 2019

To say I was ready for summer would be an understatement. I was ready to rip off the band-aid of the past couple of weeks and plunge head first into swimming, hanging with friends, and beach trips. I had begun walking regularly by now, and these activities were now accessible.

One day, Katie and I were planning on leaving the house to go to our friend's pool club for the day.

"Bye mom! See you later," Katie called while running out and slamming the car door. My mom waved goodbye to Katie casually, then turned to me and cast a discerning look as I stood patiently waiting by the door. My mom took one quick glance down at my bare legs that would be exposed to the glaring June sun and shook her head disapprovingly. I knew it would be another twenty minutes before I could leave the house.

Leaving the house had become an ordeal for me that summer. It was a ritual of preparation and precaution that made my eyes roll time and time again. At the start of the summer, I transitioned from my leggings to a tan cloth wrap that ran all the way from my ankle to my knee. It provided much-needed compression and tried to reduce the swelling that had travelled down to my ankle. The wrap looked something like an 80's leg warmer.

After I had more time to heal and the swelling had decreased, came "the patch," a jumbo-sized square latex band-aid. I pasted two of them on my leg to cover my larger wounds. I tried to smooth out the band-aids so that they were flush with my skin, but placed at such awkward angles, the patches would peel away from my skin around the corners when I moved.

More than the hideous sight beneath, there was something else I tried to avoid by wearing the patches: zinc sunscreen. Blindingly bright and white, the zinc sunscreen provided the maximum sun protection that my mom and doctor insisted upon. If I did not take care of my scars now, they would remain the dark brown color forever. However, what zinc sunscreen gains in functionality, it lacks in appearance. The sunscreen does not rub in, and it leaves a thick, goopy residue all over my leg which sharply contrasts my tanned skin. It was humiliating.

As a result, I chose the patch and in vain tried to hide my newly forming scars. That day at my friend Amelia's pool club, I stood awkwardly watching the rest of the kids dipping into the pool and cooling off. I sat isolated and dry, watching the scene play out as though it was through a television screen.

But I could not expose my leg. I never dared to do anything that would compromise the patch that was barely hiding my wounds underneath. So I made up excuses to not go in the pool: *oh, the wounds can't get wet, even though they could. I'm not feeling too well today, I'll swim another time,* even when I craved the feeling of the cool water on my skin.

I was just too afraid of the consequences: of having to rip the band-aid off. What I didn't realize for a while, was that the band-aid was not doing much to hide my wounds. Shaped like a perfect square, the band-aids did not conform or mold to the complex and windy curves of my bites. It became slippery when I wore sunscreen, sometimes leaving the patch hanging half-way off my leg.

I was too embarrassed to peel off the entire bandage, and I was keenly aware of the confused and disturbed glances as bystanders viewed the grotesque sight underneath. I went through boxes and boxes of bandages, but they could not fully hide my wounds underneath: the flaming red scars and bruised skin snaked out into the open and could not be hid by a simple piece of latex.

I wanted to slip back into normalcy, but people continued to ask what happened, and the band-aid had almost the opposite effect that I wanted. It was like a magnet, drawing stares.

Others were not as forward and didn't ask questions, but their eyes always gave them away. I became familiar with the feeling of being watched, and I could sense the wandering gaze of eyes trailing down my legs. Most of the time, people noticed when they were standing behind me, but I could still sense gawking stares. They caused a shiver up my spine. Kids especially were entranced by my injury: it wasn't the typical sprained ankle or torn ACL that is so common in a town filled with athletes.

After a while, I had become so tired of repeating the exhausting events of the dog attack that I would simply say "it's a long story." It started to work and people moved on. But even after the news had gotten around town, to friends, and to the tennis world, I would have strangers question me all the time. I wondered why they even cared, but I guess that's just the human mind: always looking for peculiarities and entertainment.

June 30th, 2019

One morning, I strolled down the steps in my house. Unlike my sister, who walks with heavy echoing thumps, my feet patted down the stairs with a light, imperceptible noise. I had just found online a gorgeous new purple dress back in stock that I had been longing for. It was a beautiful eyelet fabric, a long maxi dress that draped all the way to the ground, and I imagined it would flow in the summer wind. Conveniently, it was long enough to cover my left leg and the scars beneath. It was more expensive than the typical things I bought, but I pictured myself twirling in the purple dress like nothing had ever happened.

Walking down the stairs, I dreamt about the fun things I would do that day now that I could walk, and I relished in the carefree nostalgia of summer.

"We need to talk to someone about this, it can't be right," I heard my mom whisper to my dad confused. I could hear the pitchy break in her voice when something is bothering her, when she is upset. I can always tell from the tone in her voice when she is on the verge of tears. She always claims I'm making it up.

"For a two hour surgery? That cannot be right. Insurance has to cover it, she didn't intentionally get attacked by a dog. This is not our fault." My dad chimed in, still speaking in a similar hushed voice. I could hear the concern in his voice, and I could envision their eyes squinting with concern.

After hearing the word "dog", a shock went through my body and I paused on the stairs: I knew they were talking about me. The independent, fiery side of me beat through my chest, and I longed to burst down the stairs and enter the conversation. I felt that I was involved, that I needed to hear this, even if we were struggling financially. I couldn't deal with the oblivion of being shielded from the truth, of being told that everything was alright when we were falling apart at the seams.

"The owner is twenty years old. I've spoken to the lawyer, we're not going to get any money. We can't sue the town, they're not going to hold the girl watching the dog liable, and we're stuck with a $32,000 bill and have to pay the consequences," the exasperation in my mom's voice penetrated the wall dividing us and seeped through my skin. Guilt wracked my body like an animal because it suddenly seemed like it was all my fault. My parents would have to pay for my twin sister and my college in just over two years, they didn't need yet another financial burden. My hands shook a little, and my body felt cold.

My dad laughed sarcastically, "Well that $75 leash fine surely made up for everything Emily's been through."

Instead of continuing downstairs, I turned the other way and tiptoed back up to my room without a peep. I sat down with my laptop. Slowly, I opened the lid and deleted the tab with the beautiful purple dress.

July 3, 2019

Like every year, we were in Pittsburgh at my grandparents' house for the fourth of July. Filled with festive traditions like the family wiffle ball game, driveway fireworks, and manhunt, this holiday was always one of my favorites. We spend everyday outdoors, soaking in the summer sun. My Mom and I agreed that this would be the perfect time to get back on the tennis court.

At this point, I had been walking for over a month, but I still had done very limited exercise. My go-to fitness workout was always to hit some tennis balls--I loathed the gym or going on a run--and I knew that sooner or later I had to get back in the saddle. Or I never would.

It was just my mom and I on a sweltering summer night when I took my first steps back on a court. We played at my mom's high school, on the very courts where she grew up and fell in love with the game. It was quiet, and no one was around. I expected there to be some rush of emotion or grand entrance when I unlocked and opened the wire gate to the tennis courts. But there was no symphony or trumpets to announce my return to the game. Instead, it felt normal. It felt like I had never missed a moment, like I had fallen right back into step where I was before.

I scanned the court cautiously and took note of everything nearby. There were a few kids playing soccer on the fields down below. There was a work truck parked near the school entrance. I glanced around the court, and I meticulously shut every gate. I ran across all six courts, even to the gate furthest away from me and shut it tight. There was a resounding click as the lock fixed into place. Just as it should be.

Then, we started to play. My mom and I were both rusty from lack of practice, but it felt comfortable to hold the grip of the racket in my hand. I moved the tough strings with my fingers, allowing them to bounce back into place. I was happy to feel the vibrations as the racket made contact with the ball, and I sensed the blood course through my body when I ran to retrieve it (more accurately, I *tried* to retrieve the ball. I was not fully ready to run or move yet).

Regardless, I felt back in sync. Even though my arms ached from simply holding up the racket and my feet did not bounce as energetically as they did before, I felt at home. It was hard to believe that the last time I had been on a court was the very day that the dog attack occurred. It was hard to believe that the last match I played was on senior day when I had no inkling of the events to come. It was comical to think that I had believed I could be back in time for states in the beginning of June.

"So, when can I get back to tournaments?" I asked my mom seriously. She laughed, thinking I was joking. My mom walked to the net and beckoned me to come forward too. This is where we always had many important talks, face to face on the tennis court when we stopped playing because something was just too crucial not to say.

"Aw, Emily. We don't need to worry about that right now. Let's get you back into shape and hit a bit more first. There's no rush. You know I'd love to see you get back out there. I missed watching you play the whole postseason this year, and you know I love to watch you play tennis, probably more than you even love playing."

As she said this, I heard a car door slam somewhere behind me. Almost immediately, the perfect bubble that we had existed in on the tennis court was invaded. The chatter of conversation floated through the air towards us. A car door beeped, and I heard the clack of a latch being lifted. The gate on the opposite side of the net, my mom's side, screeched open. I distinctly remember that sound echoing throughout the air, as the tennis courts seemed to have imploded, breaking down the barrier between the rest of the world. I backed away from the net slowly, keeping my eyes trained on the open gate. I had never felt so exposed.

But it was not the people I was concerned about, but the dog tugging on the leash held by a young girl. An innocent, small gray dog that most would have found cute. I probably would have, before everything happened. Two months after the dog attack, I was used to seeing dogs. They were all over town, and I had become acutely aware of them everywhere I went--owners walking them down the street, families playing fetch at the park, dogs running by themselves through the woods next to my house. Dogs stood out to me, whereas before they faded into the background.

But worse than seeing this dog that day, was seeing a dog on the tennis court: a mirror image of what had happened before. That's what bothered me: I was not afraid of tennis courts, and up to that point I had tolerated the presence of dogs. But to see both of these things brought together wracked my whole body. It transported me back to the day of the dog attack.

Innocent as the small, fluffy dog in Pittsburgh appeared, I could not remove the graphic, bloody images from my head. I could not get the feeling of being pulled and torn out of my head. *It's on a leash*, I repeated to myself over and over like a mantra. I remember the intense fear rushing through my body and gathering in my throat.

As the family walked across the tennis court my mom and I were on, (we were currently paused and stood still with bated breath) the dog tugged at the young girl's leash and his paws scratched at the concrete court. My grip on my racket tightened until my hands turned red, and this time, I would not let go of my racket. That's when the girl dropped the leash. And I ran.

Dismayed, my mom ran in the opposite direction towards the dog and the owners. She urged them to use a leash, and she quickly explained my story. A mother lion protecting her cub, she confronted what I feared most.

It's all a blur what happened then, but I remember running off the court, pulling on the car door, yanking it open, and collapsing inside.

It was confusing. What are the odds that a dog was at the tennis court I was playing on the first time I went back to tennis? I don't recall a dog ever being on a tennis court before--besides that day in May, of course. I wished it weren't true, but irony seems to be a part of this story.

My breathing had finally slowed, and I clutched my tennis racket in my hand. My mind swam back to that horrifying day that I could not and would not forget. I checked that the car doors were safely shut and locked.

May 11, 2019

It's funny how there are many days in our lives that we have forgotten. These memories have made our lives the way that they are today, but most of the time we look back on these moments and they are fractured. They are little fragments of time fading and morphing as our lives go on. They are often lost in the entangled web of consciousness that makes up our story.

That's what makes traumatic memories different from the rest: more than a year later, I can still look back on May 11th and picture that day with perfect clarity. It is forever frozen in time- - a photograph, a snapshot where I can still recall the feelings, sights, and sounds I heard that day. I remember each thing I did, each little motion and small minutiae as though I can press play and re-watch the scene unfold in my head. I reckon it's a day I'll never forget.

That morning I had woken up early and was thrilled at the prospect of the day ahead of me: I could finally drive. I drove to my favorite little coffee shop in town, Caffe Nero, and I worked for about two hours on my English paper. I sat nestled in a small corner booth, energized by the coffee running through my veins. I tapped away at my laptop and flipped through my book peacefully. There was little care to be had at the time, and I was relishing in the first steps of independence that were granted to me in the form of a car key.

I was wrapping up my paper when I heard the *beep* of the text coming into my phone. I groaned as I read the message from my mom:

Remember, Katie can't take her lesson today, and you are playing tennis with Lana. Don't be late!

I felt I needed to study more, but with the start of our county tournament, FCIAC's, approaching, I knew that I had to practice. I knew that I wanted to win and that my team needed me to be in the best shape possible. So of course I had agreed to go. How could I have known?

I left Caffe Nero with a renewed sense of purpose and a skip in my step. I chose my own music, cranked up the volume slightly louder than my mom approved, rolled down the windows, and made my way home.

Driving through town with the wind whipping through the windows and messing up my hair, I felt like I had reached the epitome of what it meant to be a teenager--on the edge of adulthood and responsibility, yet still relishing in the carefree existence of childhood. I finally felt that cliche, glorified feeling of freedom after getting one's license.

After a quick change into tennis clothes, I reluctantly passed on the car to my sister. I rolled my eyes at the thought of having my mom drive me to tennis: I was a licensed driver, for pete's sake! Yet I hopped inside the passenger seat of my mom's car anyways, feeling slightly defeated giving up the freedom I had so recently earned. My mom drove me to the Cove Beach Park in Stamford where I was playing tennis as scheduled. I'd played there before several times. The sight of the four fenced-in courts perched above the basketball court brought back memories of challenging practices and taxing days.

After slamming the car door shut and a quick wave, I skipped up the hill and past the basketball court with a sense of excitement. It was the most stunning day, sunny and 75 degrees with a cool breeze that was a glimpse into the summer that was to come. Despite the perfect setting, the courts and park itself were surprisingly empty: there were very few cars in the parking lot, and the typical laughter of children was absent.

But most shocking, was that no one was playing basketball next to the tennis courts. Normally, the basketball court was filled with kids, teens, and adults alike shooting hoops and having a good time. The court was always packed, people would even watch on the bleachers, and a pick-up game was almost always happening. A sunny day in May seemed to be the perfect time for these kinds of activities, but the basketball court stood empty. Completely silent. This was something that my mom mentioned that puzzled me later: why weren't there people there that day? If someone was there, particularly one of the strong, adult athletes who could have intervened, I don't think the events would have unfolded the same way.

But at the time this didn't strike me as odd, and I didn't even notice. I was simply excited to see one of my coaches/hitting partners, Lana, whom I hadn't seen for months. With her perky ponytail, and athletic tennis-player build, Lana always reminded me of a touring professional. From Ukraine, her life had mirrored other tennis stars like Maria Sharapova, who moved to the United States for opportunities and to advance her career. I always loved hitting with Lana, and she was the perfect person to practice with to prepare for the FCIAC tournament.

I opened the metal gate and slipped inside the tennis courts. I left the door slightly ajar and became absorbed in the realm of tennis the minute I stepped in. On the tennis court, I felt a heightened sense of focus, and for a brief time everything else seemed to slip away. With no one else playing that day, we had the luxury of choosing any of the courts. We chose the first court, even though the net seemed slightly high. Higher nets are always better to practice on anyway.

I remember the practice started like any other, and I was relaxed and at ease. I ran my lap around the court and completed my warm-up stretches with the familiarity and confidence of someone who had done this their whole life--which, I virtually had. I tucked my hair into my typical high pony-tail and smoothed out the fly-a-ways. With a final tug to tighten my shoelaces, I was ready to play. Routine complete.

As we warmed up "mini tennis" at the service line, like always Lana and I chatted about school, my family, and the normal things in life. I gushed exuberantly about my author study project in English that I had worked on all morning. I recounted the important events of the past few weeks: my near-perfect tennis season at number one singles and the success of my team up through senior day a few days prior.

I was happy in that moment; there was a stirring anticipation in my chest for the post-season which was still yet to come. This was the most exciting part of the tennis season--now each match counted more than ever, and we had our eyes set on the coveted FCIAC and State Championship titles, which had elusively slipped between our fingers the year before. We had won second place against our rival, Staples, but we were hungry for redemption. Goosebumps dotted my arms even thinking about it. I had always craved that idyllic, come from behind win: I loved being the underdog more than anything, because the win was always more satisfying. Everyone seems to love that perfect redemption story, especially in sports.

After our warm-up, we moved back to the baseline. Lana hit deep and powerfully into the court, and after only a few minutes I was already breathing heavily. Back and forth the yellow ball soared across the net like a glowing orb. I pushed myself to move my feet rapidly and track down every ball. *Split-step, sprint, smack, recover. Split-step, sprint, smack, recover.* Over and over I followed this pattern, beating every ball back and letting none pass by me.

During a brief pause between points, I walked to the back fence and shut my eyes. The sweat dripped down my forehead and trickled down my face before plopping to the court below. With my eyes shut, I could almost forget I was even there. I imagined I was playing for the state title. I was down a set, but this was the position I always wanted to be in-- you could never count me out when I was behind.

I turned to the left and I saw one of my teammates shaking the hand of her opponent: she had just won. The heavy sound of clapping and the intangible weight of excitement surrounded me. I turned to the right and I saw my sister zoned into her match, a grimace on her face, and grunting like the classic tennis player. I looked down at my hands and they were red and raw from the friction holding my tennis racket. The other team and their parents jeered at me and shouted until their voices cracked from the other side of the fence. I wanted to yell back at them, but I bit my lip instead.

I blinked and opened my eyes to see the black, wrought-iron fence of the Cove Beach tennis courts. In that moment I could have sworn I had seen what my life would be like in a little over two weeks' time. I turned around and strode back to the baseline, bouncing on my toes and ready for the next point to begin.

It was not long into the practice, probably only about fifteen minutes or so, when I first noticed the dog. I remember seeing a flash of white race around the black fence and the light-hearted sound of barking. From outside the fence, the dog ran back and forth between Lana's side and mine repeatedly before I realized that it was entranced with the tennis ball. Each time the glowing orb would fly back and forth, the dog would change its course of direction as if captivated by a spell. Like a puppet, the dog was pulled back and forth by the fuzzy yellow tennis ball.

When the point would stop, the dog settled down briefly, only to bark energetically when the point began again. At first it was almost comical, it seemed like the dog was eager for a game of fetch. We continued playing, thinking that at some point the owner would appear to take care of his dog. But no one ever came.

After a long few minutes of rapid chasing, the dog padded over to the gate where I had entered. I was closest to the gate, with Lana on the opposite side of the net, and the dog ran through onto the court, jumping excitedly on top of me. I was shocked at the impact as the dog reared onto his hind legs and pushed his paws against my stomach and legs. He seemed like a dog excited to meet a new person, and at the time I had brushed it off as a playful gesture.

But I did sense something different in this dog--something more aggressive rather than innocent. Maybe it was the determination in the dog or the struggle for the ball that I held in my left hand. Maybe it was the forcefulness of the jump that nearly knocked me backwards. Maybe it was the fact that after giving the dog a hesitant pet on the head, the dog persisted and forced himself higher until his paws were scratching against legs, my stomach, almost reaching my chin. I gave a slight shove and the dog finally settled down and dropped back onto all fours.

It was not until I had finally relieved the weight of the dog off of me that I noticed the rough, red scratches lining up and down my legs where the dog had jumped. From that small encounter, that dog had already imprinted itself on my body.

The white dog continued to wander around the court, padding in a circle. Looking curiously around the park, I could not see anyone. His owner was nowhere to be found. This ordeal lasted around five minutes, and we had paused our tennis for the time being until we could guide this dog off the court. I watched Lana on the other side of the net. Timidly, she hesitated and seemed not to know how to act around the dog. I could tell that she was frightened even when the dog was calm.

I took matters into my own hands and ushered the dog to the gate in the right hand corner of the tennis courts, nearest to me. He resisted and continued to turn left and right as though looking for someone. Finally, the dog slipped through the gate which I carefully shut so that we could continue playing.

It was not a typical gate with one swinging door that you could swing and shut tightly. Instead, it consisted of two swinging panels that were attached to either side of the fence. I swung them both shut, but I felt a pit in my stomach grow when I realized something: the gate was broken.

I fiddled with the fence, trying to see if I had shut it correctly or if I could push the two sides closer to one another. There was a latch hanging from one of the sides of the gate, but it was broken and falling off. It could not stretch the gap between both doors of the gate. I wished that I could stretch the doors, and like a rubber band they could expand to meet one another and shut tightly. But this was impossible. So, I pushed the two doors of the gate as far forward as I could, even grinding the metal into the concrete to test how far they could swing. I would have to be satisfied with this.

I stepped away and noted the six inches of empty space between the gate doors. Turning around, I jogged back to the baseline to continue playing, but I was keenly aware of the presence of the white dog growling outside the tennis court gate. As we started to hit again, our balls flew back and forth with resounding *pops!*

Like clockwork, the dog began barking erratically and running back and forth in a frenzy. He circled the tennis courts with an intense ferocity, darting so fast I could barely spot the dog. I felt surrounded, cornered. Finally, he arrived back at the gate that I had just meticulously tried to shut. The playful barking he had made seconds before morphed into a low-pitched, primal growl. It seemed like a predator waiting to attack its prey.

He stuck his head through the six inch gap that was my fortress's weakness. Growling and shoving his body through that gap, the dog's face changed and now revealed beady red eyes that narrowed in my direction. I could only watch with astonishment as it twisted its body and thrust itself further and further into the tennis court. Each desperate, angry movement of the dog rattled the metal gate. I squinted at the gap, *there's no way he can fit.*

At this point we had stopped playing, and my eyes remained trained on the gate and the dog trying to infiltrate it. With a final grunt and a push, he was through. With my eyes locked on the dog, it charged head on and sprinted towards me. I couldn't run, I couldn't move. I was frozen and powerless as the white dog opened its mouth and latched onto my leg.

Despite this aggressive movement, when the dog's jaw made contact with my leg, I assumed that he was licking me playfully. But when I tried to twist my leg away and shake the dog off, he remained firm. My jaw dropped when I saw the first trickle of red blood slowly slide down my leg. That's when I realized that the dog was not licking me happily, he was devouring his prey. In disbelief, I stared at my leg and watched the gruesome sight as the dog buried his head into my lower left leg.

With this recognition, I felt the first slivers of pain as the dog sank his teeth deeper and deeper into my skin. I cried out for help, but to no avail, it felt as though I was screaming underwater, like I had made no sound. I whipped my head anxiously left and right, screaming out for the owner of the dog who was nowhere to be found.

I remember Lana shaking with horror and fear on the other side of the net. She stood frozen in time, wracked with uncertainty and awe. Paralyzed with fear from the dog, she rushed to the fence on her side of the court and yelled until a young girl finally ran onto the court. She could not have been more than my age, but I assumed she was the dog's owner. The leash hung limply from her hand, a powerful weapon that could have once saved me and could have prevented this disaster in the first place. It now was rendered useless, and she dropped it to the ground.

She hesitated as she stood in the open doorway to the court and began screaming for the dog to come: "Tyson!! Tyson come!! Stop it, no, no, no, no!!" Her voice became cracked and raw from screaming, but her voice was not enough to register any change in the dog.

As the dog tore through my skin, grappling to get a strong hold, he made more and more bites on my leg. When the dog finally found a strong position, he maintained his grip and pulled violently on my leg. With a tearing motion, he latched onto my leg and dug deeper and deeper into that one spot, biting through flesh and closing in on my tendon.

His bark was replaced by something more sinister. I could hear the low rumbling growl as he cut deeper into me. It was the most feral and animalistic sound I had ever heard--that of a wolf, not a pet. He was hungry. Something had changed in the core of that dog: he was not a loveable house pet, but a violent, relentless assailant. He had abandoned all the decent qualities of a domestic dog and wore a new cloak--a wild, vicious one.

From the other side of the court, Lana began firing tennis balls like rockets. She reluctantly stood closer to the net, but she remained rooted on the other side of the court, afraid of the chaos that ensued on my side. The net was her protection, and our two worlds diverged on opposite ends of the court. I could tell she was hardly keeping herself together, and tears and exasperation coated her face. Her efforts to hit the dog with tennis balls were in vain, as most of the tennis balls missed and very few even came in the vicinity of where I was. I noticed her shaking with fear, turning left and right erratically as though the answers were written on the sides of the fence. She threw her racket and covered her face with her hands, defeated.

With Lana in no state to help me, I turned to the girl who huddled cowardly by the door, afraid of the dog that was supposed to be her responsibility. It was like I was a leper and no one wanted to come near me.

Frustrated, I searched recklessly for my racket, thinking I could hit the dog then run for safety, although I had no idea where that might be. I must have flung my racket in shock when the dog pounced, because it lay uselessly ten feet to my left. I strained against the dog and pulled in the opposite direction of him to move towards my racket. In this struggle I fell over, scraping my knees and rolling onto my back. I felt a searing pain as the dog pulled against my leg and repositioned his biting hold on my body. Instinctively, I covered my stomach to protect myself and heaved my body off the ground. Even through this all, the dog remained attached, buried into my leg and transfixed by the blood like a moth to a flame.

Back on my feet, I re-evaluated my position. In agony, I realized that my racket was still at least seven feet away. I knew that I could not risk falling to the ground again and resorting to such a compromised position where the dog could grab hold of my stomach or face. The seven feet prevented me from a clean escape. It was simply too far.

At that point, I dared to peak down at my leg. I was aghast as blood flowed more steadily from my wounds. It was no longer the trickle that I first witnessed, but it was gushing down my leg. I watched in awe as my skin buckled from the tension. The more blood that gushed from my leg, the more aggressive and vicious the dog became. His growls became louder and his pulling on my leg became harder. Each tug from the dog sent me flying toward his direction. In a repetitive cycle, I fought to move the other way, but was continuously dragged back towards the sharp jaw of the dog.

My body slackened as the dog moved into a rhythm: he continued to bite and tear at my body relentlessly, almost in a robotic way. I sensed no ease in his tearing. Nonetheless, the dog's fierce growling started to fade into the background. Instead of looking at the gory sight that was my leg, I was drawn by some intangible force to crane my neck and look at the sky.

As I took in the beautiful May day, I started to relax. Taking these few moments, I watched the clouds slowly, imperceptibly drift through the sky. I looked up at the foliage of the trees shading the tennis courts--they rustled softly in the wind. It was nice and warm, and for a few seconds I could almost forget what was going on. I felt my body give in. I felt at peace.

I don't know how long I was mesmerized in this position, but suddenly I stirred from this dream-like state. I think it was around then that I made a choice. I made the choice to fight, because I realized that no one else was coming. I was jarred by this recognition, and I grew conscious of the fact that I was losing a lot of blood. But the dog was not losing steam. Despite the improbability and the sheer absurdity of this situation, I knew that this fiasco would soon become a matter of life and death.

I snapped my head away from the sky. I zoned in on my leg and the situation at hand. That's when I started to call the shots. There was no way that I could push this dog off of me with my bare hands. But the problem was I had no weapon. There was no way that I was safe on this court. Yet we were at a park full of open space, and I had no car to go to. I knew that I was going to have to run. I did not know if I even *could* run, but I knew that I was going to have to.

"Call 911 Lana! Go!" I shouted, while simultaneously beckoning the young girl over. I thought if just maybe she could grab her dog and hold him back we would be able to wrestle him off of me. My sinewy stature could not compete with the ferocity of the dog in a trance: like a wolf, he was honing in on the kill. He had it set in his mind and locked tight in his jaw.

"Come grab your dog please. Please come, please help me." I begged her, even as I saw her shaking in horror by the door, not wanting to enter into the dark abyss of the court.

"It's not my dog, it's not my dog, I don't know what to do," she uttered repeatedly. Nonetheless, I continued to shout for her to come closer, to at least try to grab the collar of the dog. I had no plan in mind for what would happen when she trekked across the several feet that divided us. At that point, my mind was detached from my body, but I continued to move with a renewed sense of urgency and purpose. Each twist of my body and flick of my hand was deliberate, and my body filled with a surge of energy.

I clutched onto the girl's shirt as she stumbled closer. I was hanging on, not for emotional support, but to steady myself as the dog continued to tear at my leg. Up close, it was clear that the girl was only a few years older than myself with wide teary eyes and a look of panic slapped across her face. She was older, but in those moments she transformed into a frightened young girl. She was afraid, and tears streamed down her cheeks.

Meanwhile, my eyes remained dry. They remained locked on the raging dog in front of me. My senses were heightened in that moment, and blood pumped faster through my body. My breathing quickened, air raging in and out of my lungs.

I could tell that there was no way this girl could grab the dog. With each step closer to me, she whimpered at the blood, and she gave me a saddened look as though I was already a lost cause. Each time she reluctantly leaned in closer and reached for his collar, she quickly ripped her hand away to avoid the thrashing of the dog. I knew that she had no power over this dog. Only one thing did.

I glanced down and saw a flash of yellow as one of the tennis balls Lana had hurled had landed only inches from my feet. I leaned over and snatched the ball in my hands. Without hesitation

I shoved the tennis ball underneath the dog's mouth as he was leaning in for another bite. I pushed the dog off of me, and I ran. And I didn't look back.

I didn't wait to see if the dog grabbed onto the ball or if it even made it into his mouth. That fuzzy yellow tennis ball, the orb that had once transfixed the dog had been my distraction. Then I made my escape. With a piercing sense of urgency, I ran as fast as I could off of the tennis courts and burst through the gate, leaving the doors flung wide open.

At that moment I had to assume that the dog was chasing me, so I didn't dare turn around. My body propelled me forward, and I sprinted on pure adrenaline with only one thought in mind: to put as much distance between the dog and me as possible. My ponytail hung loose and my hair flew into my face. A surge of energy burst through my body and seemed to push me forward, telling me *keep going, keep going.*

My legs pumped back and forth as I raced downhill, past the basketball court and into the near-empty parking lot. As I ran, my eyes searched frantically for my car, feeling a sense of relief that I could finally drive, and this token of freedom would save me. This was instantly replaced by a pit of doom as I remembered that my mom had dropped me off and Lana had walked to the tennis courts: there was no car to serve as my refuge. There were no buildings in sight, and if I waited too long to find a safe place, the dog would find me.

That's when I spotted the Toyota Camry, nestled a few spots over from the basketball court. I eyed the open window, and I found my exit.

While some might find it foolish to tumble head-first into a stranger's car, it was certainly the lesser of two evils. I didn't think twice about my decision to enter the car, and I didn't even question my body's ability to jump through the window. I ran and leaped through the window, dragging my leg along the side of the car and tumbling into the passenger seat. I landed awkwardly and heaved my legs through the car so that the dog could not follow me.

I could hardly comprehend what I had done and how frightening I must have seemed when I swiveled around in the front seat and faced the driver. I locked eyes with a sweet woman with a warm round face and eyes full of worry--not fear.

"I'm so sorry, I'm so sorry. A dog attacked me while I was playing tennis just now. I got away, and I ran. I didn't know if the dog was chasing me, so I saw your window and I leaped to safety," I panted from exhaustion.

"Shhh, don't worry, I'll help you. Let me call 911," the kind woman whispered, stroking my arm as she fumbled around for tissues. She handed them to me and directed me to cover up my wound and attempt to stop the bleeding. I hadn't realized that I had tracked blood into her car and all over her seats and window. I felt so sorry that I had pushed my problems onto this sweet, innocent woman enjoying her Saturday.

Even with the sharp pain solidifying on my leg and with chills wrapping my body, I breathed in and out. I watched the cars pass on the street, hoping for one to be my mom's. I felt the cool air from the air conditioning tickle my nose. I heard sirens in the distance. I told myself that I was going to be okay. As I breathed, I started to believe it.

I only learned later that the dog that attacked me was a pit bull and that the true owner was away. I only learned later that my mom had arrived at the tennis courts and was only feet away as I waited anxiously in the ambulance before it left for the hospital. Looking back, I'm amazed at how composed I was in these moments. I was calm and coherent, because I knew that I needed to be in order to protect myself. No one else was going to do it for me.

I am still very proud of saving myself that day, but I'll always remember jumping through that woman's window to safety. I had infiltrated her life, but she could not have been kinder. I could have hopped into any stranger's car, that of a serial killer or a robber, but I learned later that the woman whose car I had hopped into happened to be a nurse. I'm not sure if it was a stroke of good luck amongst all the madness or the mysterious inner-workings of fate, but I was safe. This woman who heals for a living had in-part rescued me, simply by leaving her window open.

Part II
Opening The Gate (Healing)

A Blend of Dates on My Journey

It's not a secret that I've struggled with some form of post-traumatic stress disorder. Some of my closest friends witnessed this on a summer night at my friend Kinga's house with her dog. We were cleaning up from dinner when Maggie (the dog) came trotting outside. A happy-go-lucky golden retriever whom I have known for a while, she was quickly energized by the sight of food before her still lying on the table. In particular, she spotted a piece of pizza dangling from my sister's hand, who sat next to me.

Maggie started barking wildly and running in circles, then sank her teeth into the pizza. When Kinga tried to grab her, Maggie started growling in a low, angry tone. I was wracked with emotion as my mind flooded back to May 11th, when I heard that nearly identical sound being uttered from the dog as he attacked me. It was not the barking that triggered me, but that bellowing, animalistic growl.

I shifted away in my seat and bit my tongue. I started shaking uncontrollably as I watched in horror as Maggie opened her mouth and surrounded Kinga's arm, teeth enclosing around her as though she were about to take a bite. Maggie would not let go and continued to jump up on top of her owner, whom she was supposed to be loyal to and love.

My friends watched with a mix of confusion and concern as I whimpered and tears welled up in my eyes and overflowed. I stood up abruptly and pushed away from the table, clutching to the sides of the porch. With clouded eyes, I walked away, because I couldn't be there: the sounds and sights were too poignant and transported me back to that horrible day. I wanted to run away as far as I could.

That's some PTSD right there," one of my friends commented, a sad look on his face. I never pictured myself as someone who could have PTSD. I thought that was reserved for soldiers in battle.

I blamed the things that I thought I could control--the physical elements that could have protected me from the horrible accident. I turned to the gate. If only that metal gate had shut tightly, I would not have endured such a traumatizing event. If only that metal gate had been fused together instead of leaving a six-inch gap, I would not have suffered from the brutal pain of my injury and the continuation of nerve pain that would haunt me for a year after the dog attack. If only that metal gate had locked tightly and done its job, I would not have the frightening memories and fears that I lock away deep in my mind. That gate was the last thing protecting me from the dog, the last defense that I had relied on to keep me safe. I started locking myself in and throwing away the key. I chose to shut the gates in my life.

I was waiting. Waiting for something to happen, some divine intervention that would set the balance of the universe straight. Something that would avenge me for all the pain and psychological warfare this freak accident had wreaked on me.

In retrospect, I realize that I carried this toxic mindset for quite some time: I felt that after all I had suffered and been through, I deserved something in return. Some good fortune or happy circumstance, some tangible success that would make the pain seem worth it. I think we idealize our world as a place that works as a balance: when something burdens us, there will be some positive force or retribution to counteract the load. We squint and look for these silver linings, expecting them to be there.

I healed the most psychologically the day I realized I didn't *deserve* anything. The events that make up our lives are often completely random, and there is no solid reason why bad things happen to good people. We're all just floating in the waves of fate, flailing and trying to keep our heads above water until one day we learn how to swim.

For some time, I was waiting for the silver lining to mysteriously and suddenly appear, and to make the struggle worth it. But over time it became clear that I was not going to receive some tangible medal for my sufferings. The one thing I could do is heal, and this thought became very therapeutic.

I had longed for some guardian angel to appear and to make sense of the world for me. So when I realized nothing was coming, I became my own translator trying to process the complicated language of circumstance that slapped me in the face. I thought a lot about my trauma, dreamed about it, talked about it, and---most importantly---wrote about it. My thoughts came rushing out of my mind, relieving the tangled knot of trauma. With these very words on this very page, everything seems a little lighter.

July 2019

I dragged my fingers down my leg, and I slowed down as I reached the back of my knee and my calf. Carefully, I traced the jagged, bumpy mounds that make up my scars. I shut my eyes, and I felt the rise and fall of the thick scars like mountains, although they barely extended above the surface of my skin. Now they make up the fabric of my skin. My scars.

At this point in time, my scars were a reddish-purple color, thrown haphazardly over my lower left leg. Particularly in the back of my leg, behind my knee where the most trauma had occurred, I was fascinated by the scars. In the back, my scars were thick and fleshy. Ribbed with stretch lines and in oval-like shapes of all different sizes, my scars looked like ugly leeches stuck to my skin and seeping the blood out of me. But I loved them, nonetheless. I joked that they were my purple caterpillars, hanging onto my leg and keeping me company.

My scars painted a clear picture of what had happened to me: you could see the jagged angle and sharp, uneven cuts that were made from the dog's jaw. My scars were a physical reminder of what I had been through. They were the manifestation of the horror that I had endured and survived.

It is interesting where my scars are located: nestled behind my knee and concentrated on the inside of my calf, my scars are not visible when you face me head-on. Yes, some small brown lines and bruise-looking marks peek around the corners, but they are virtually invisible from head-on and from my view looking down. Shielded from the true extent of my injuries and scars, I could almost forget that the scars are even there. Almost.

I became keenly aware of their presence that summer as I worked in the golf shop where my dad is the head golf professional. My work consists of ringing up sales, answering the phone, fixing clothing displays, etc. Each day I wear golf clothes to work (even though I'm not much of a golfer, to my dad's remiss). My "uniform" consists of a sleeveless collared top, sneakers, and a golf skirt. Golf skirts are conservative; however, they hang just inches above the knee, and therefore they are inches away from covering my wounds. In fact, the skirt perfectly frames where my scars begin, and it almost draws attention to my left calf.

Despite this, I was still surprised that summer when club members would notice my leg. I was perplexed by how my injury had become such common knowledge. My story had spread quickly. Talking about my injury had become as common as helping customers pick out new golf clothes.

To be perfectly honest, this didn't bother me. People genuinely cared about me. They checked in constantly to see how I was doing and listened to my story with bated breath. Telling my story was invaluable at times; I was able to talk about what had happened without any fear. I came to terms with what had happened.

It also became a routine where I would come around the counter at work and do a little spin to show off my healing scars to the members, our customers. I was proud of the progress I was making, and regardless of the concern and pity of the viewers, I knew that my leg was healing. It looked better than it did the day before and the day before that.

My experiences at my job strengthened me. What took me off guard were the people who didn't know my story. A new friend I made over the summer. A waiter at a restaurant. A random stranger on the street. Not to mention the unwarranted stares and the downward glances that people would think were slick, but I could always feel crawling down my skin. It was the people that didn't know me and didn't know the improvement that threw me off.

"Is that dirt on your leg?"

"What are all of those bruises on your leg? Are you okay?"

"What happened there?"

"What's that white stuff spread all over your leg? Is that sunscreen?"

Their comments stung more than others. It was a constant reminder that I didn't look completely normal anymore.

I've always been a neat-freak. I crave when I am clean, organized, and productive. The first thing I do when I wake up in the morning is make my bed. I always set out my clothes for the next day the night before. I keep a schedule of tasks to get done each day, and my color-coded planner is my best friend. I cannot stand when my room is messy and I don't do well with surprises. I'm a person who always has to have a plan. When I was really little and my parents surprised us with going to Disney World, I started crying. Not just because I was happy, but because I was not prepared and it caught me off guard.

My personality is the antithesis of my scars. Chaotic, uneven, messy, and unplanned, my injuries were clear opponents to my very existence. Instead of a neat, polished look, my legs are filled with battle scars and colors of all different shades.

As I struggled to shave my legs every time after the attack, I moved slower and more cautious than I had before. I squirted mounds of shaving cream into my palm and lathered my legs so that every inch was covered, save for the area that contained the most scarring. Slowly, I pulled the razor up my leg, moving inch by inch up the curve of my calf. I paused when I reached a fork in the road: I turned my razor slowly and weaved my way through the thick scars, past the rough patches, and over the curves and dips of my leg. I hesitated when I reached the dimple of my leg--the dip that was never there before. Now every time I flex my leg muscles, the dimple deepens into a chasm. I pick my razor up and move on to the other side of my leg: the smooth, easy-to-shave side.

I recalled in eighth grade when I was still relatively inexperienced at shaving. I went too fast and with too little shaving cream. As I dragged the razor briskly up my leg, I felt a sharp tearing, and I could feel a small layer of skin ripping away. Blood rose to the surface of my skin and trickled down my leg. More blood kept rising and the gushing would not stop. I remember calling out for my mom, who rushed in and helped me clean the cut and wrap my ankle in multiple bandages. "It'll probably leave behind a small scar," she said, reassuring me that I would be okay. Back then, that tan thin line had seemed so large and impeding. Back then, that tiny scar felt like a threat to my orderly world.

As much as I feel like I have ignored or forgotten the scars that are embedded in my left leg, there are always days when I think about it. If I look at myself in the mirror for a little too long or if I'm wearing shorts and am surrounded by people with perfect, unblemished legs. Ignoring the scars is simply ignoring what happened to me. That's something I don't want to do.

My scars are a reminder of what I've suffered through and where I've come from. They will always tell my story because they're not only etched into my legs but into my soul. I have to accept that they aren't going anywhere. Not even time will fully heal some of these wounds. Not even following the perfect regimen of massages, scar tape, oil, and sunscreen will erase the marks that now define me. These scars that have changed me, molded me, and have grown with me.

While others complain about their appearance, I remain happy with the way I look. My scars have become an extension of myself. I take a good hard look at them every day and admire the rich, dark brown color and the bumps and keloids that are funny to trace. These scars are purely mine, unique to me. So I embraced my scars--they are my battle scars.

August 2019

Whenever people talk about their fears, they typically boil down to a few phobias, such as heights, spiders, and clowns. For me, it was always none of the above. I thought I wasn't afraid of anything--at least not the conventional fears. I was always pretty fearless. But after the dog attack, I sensed a change. It took me a while to realize that I did have a fear: dogs. People had always asked me if I was traumatized after the dog attack, and I brushed it off. My parents asked me time and time again if I needed to talk to a professional therapist about this. I don't know if it was pride, frugality, or self-conviction--perhaps all three-- but I always said no. I could handle it.

"I'm fine," I always stated. But it was hard to reconcile that "man's best friend," had suddenly become my worst enemy. After telling people my story countless times, some sense of clarity or closure still had not resonated with me. It felt like I was trying to convince myself of a version of reality rather than truly understand what had happened. When recanting the events, people always assumed that the dog had been put down. My reply was always: "No, they didn't. I'm glad they didn't. I don't think I would have liked the burden of the dog's death on my hands. I don't really blame the dog, I blame the owner for being irresponsible."

At first, this seemed to be my classic line to please the dog lovers and to tie up the conversation with a neat bow. It was logical. It was concise. But it would be a lie to say that I harbored no resentment for what happened to me. I hated dogs for a while. I loathed them for a time and started to think that all dogs inherently carried these evil, malicious tendencies. I believed that at the core they were animals, wolves with instinctual desires to hunt and kill.

This paranoia followed me whenever I stepped outside of the comforting gates of my backyard and out into the unfenced world. While some people are claustrophobic and fear small confining spaces, it is when I am in the open that I feel the most in danger. I feel exposed, like anyone or anything can come up behind me and shock me when I least expect it. That summer, I looked left and right before leaving the protection of my house. I crept from the garage and tiptoed down the sloping driveway to our car parked at the edge of the woods. I listened for the dreaded sound of barking or a jangling collar. Sometimes it would simply be the clanging of someone's car keys and I would jump with concern. I scanned the dark foliage of the woods for any roaming animals, and I darted inside the car.

Other times when I was out in public, I purposely avoided dogs. If I saw someone walking their dog on the street, I changed positions and slipped to the other side of my friends so they could unknowingly act as a shield to any potential threat. I recall one of the early days when I was still on crutches and was waiting to be picked up early from school. I keenly spotted a brown labrador sitting with its owner on a bench outside the school. The dog blocked the pathway between the door and my mom's car, so I waited an extra few minutes until the dog was gone before I opened the door wide and left the safety of the building. Similarly, when others stooped down to pet a stranger's dog, I stood awkwardly behind, heart racing with adrenaline, my fight or flight response lurking in the event of an attack.

Even my family grew uncomfortable around dogs. If we were out to dinner and a large dog paced the streets, I watched my parents give each other knowing, rigid glances, hoping I would not notice. It was clear that my sister tensed up whenever we saw a dog on the street together. She would always bite her lip and look over at me with worry, although I would pretend not to notice, like I was unbothered by it all. This attack had touched all of our lives.

I kept most of these incidents bottled up inside. They became my little idiosyncrasies as I made my way through life. But it was clear I needed a change. Telling my story out loud to people was effective in releasing some tension that I kept bottled inside of me-- to release the emotions and confront what had happened.

Yet these stories often ignored the subtleties of the attack and my hidden fears. I formed a tangled knot in my mind that pulled and strained inside of me that consisted of everything I wanted to say but couldn't--everything I couldn't form into words.

What was more powerful for me than the talking cure was stopping and thinking, taking moments to meditate and recall what had happened. That summer I spent a lot of time outside in nature, reflecting. I realized that I rarely cried anymore, not like I used to when I was a dramatic, sensitive little kid. Instead of crying, I was wracked by a sense of uncertainty and anxiety about life: the purpose of it all.

I joke that I have existential crises every now and then, but they happen far more often than I'd like to admit. When my life seems to become a blur, I question why I stress over all the small things in life. Why is it that we obsess over being the best at a sport or having flawless grades when we are just clumps of matter stuck to an orbiting ball in an infinite space?

In these moments, I play this game called the five senses. I ground myself in nature, and I think: *What do I see? What do I hear? What do I smell? What do I taste? What do I feel?* In these moments the excess noise melts away, and I exist. I am happy. I think about what happened, and I confront the gruesome details and not just frame the perfect, succinct story for the curious individual.

Instead, when I put a pen to a piece of paper, thoughts stream out of me and dance across the page. Most of the time it isn't even as beautiful as that. Much of my writing and ideas as I wrote this book were stored on my phone on the notes app. Whenever a thought or realization gripped me, I fumbled for my phone and frantically typed bullet point notes onto the screen. I filled pages of cluttered thoughts, allowing fears to stream out of my mind.

I don't know if I refused professional therapy because I was worried about the financial burdens I had already placed on my family. It could have also been because I am fiercely independent and like to solve things on my own. I preferred to pick apart and talk about my feelings to my family, to people who really know me. Or maybe at first, I denied that the attack had any mental implications on me. I realized that was wrong on that day in Hoboken-- that day I paint in the first few lines of this book.

At times, I thought I was weak because I could not handle this difficult event in my life. I was acutely aware that there are people in the world who have suffered far worse--I was still alive, I still had all of my limbs. I second-guessed the validity of my trauma often, and I think this would surprise many people, who could clearly see the severity of the attack. Here's a piece of advice I would give to my former self: do not diminish your struggles because they look different from those of others.

August 2019

Even today, I keep my guard up around most dogs. But there's one dog in particular that I have always felt safe around, even in the early weeks after the attack. There's one dog that I have a special bond with, whom I know for certain could never hurt a fly.

As I stepped through my friend Emily Hopper's garage, I heard a soft barking in the distance--not the aggressive growl I had come to fear, but a soft, playful giggle. I turned the knob of the door, and braced for Charley to pounce on me or scratch me. Instead, I watched in awe as Charley, who had been jumping excitedly seconds before, suddenly settled down and grew quiet.

She padded over to me at the door in a calm and soothing manner. Rather than jumping up to lick my face or put her paws on my legs as other dogs would, Charley stopped when she was directly in front of me. She sat down on the hardwood floor and nuzzled up to me, warm and soft.

Charley let out a quiet whimper and rubbed her fuzzy, curly fur against my ankles as though she were whispering, *I'm sorry, you're safe with me.* Almost as if she knew.

December 2019

As days faded into weeks which transformed into months, my mind began to relax and heal. The stitches in my legs may have taken only several weeks to bind my wounds together, but my mind took longer to seal its own cuts together. I still struggled, feeling like something was wrong with me because everyone else adores dogs and I was still trying to feel comfortable around them. However, this strong negativity was counteracted by its fiercest opponent: optimism. My mind really healed when instead of resenting what happened to me, I sowed the seeds of relief, of happiness.

Instead of cowering at the sight of a dog, or feeling sad, I embraced the notion that I was "the dog attack girl." I even started to become comfortable with more of my friends' dogs, even comfortable with dogs I passed on the street.

I realized that as much as I wanted to paint the broad stroke that dogs are these dangerous, violent creatures, the reality is they truly are not. I have come to meet and know many lovable, adorable dogs. I have reconnected with the girl who always begged her parents for a puppy for Christmas.

Friends and family hypothesize that the pit bull that attacked me was probably mistreated. Maybe he was beaten by his owner. Maybe he was neglected and kept in a cage. Maybe he was trained for dog fights. There is no proof, but people can be the true aggressors at times. I start to let my walls down, and I pity the dog that hurt me. He was probably hurt himself.

Despite the massive improvement to ease my emotional scars, to be truthful, the echoes of May 11th still haunted me even seven months later. The phantom nerve pain still gripped my leg, and I had not regained full feeling. If you pinched or rubbed my left shin, I would only feel an imperceptible buzzing, but no complete sensations. My left leg was still held hostage in this way. Like if I shaved too quickly, I wouldn't even feel that I had cut myself and that blood was trickling down my leg. Random green bruises appeared on my lower left leg, I presumed from bumping into furniture without feeling any pain or truly noticing.

By December, I had made great strides. Sometimes I could almost forget that I was attacked by a dog. This was especially true when it is cold outside and so easy to cover up what happened with a pair of leggings. I know my parents are disappointed that the jagged purple-brown scars did not disappear, but I have learned to live with them. Even as they flatten and fade slightly over time, they will always be mine, my purple caterpillars.

March 6th, 2020

I glided through the lobby of the Connecticut State Capitol building. Captivated by the high-vaulted ceilings, intricate carvings, and lush marble, I felt as though I was shrinking at the hands of this important and large building.

I usually abhorred the idea of being absent from school, fearing that I would miss critical information for tests. But when Terrie Wood, our state representative, called us last minute saying she had secured a spot for me to testify, I knew this opportunity was more important than anything I could learn in the four walls of a classroom.

After my attack, I started researching and exploring on the internet: stories about other dog attacks, bites, and lawsuits. These stories varied in location from Pennsylvania to Iowa to California and ranged in age from teenagers to infants to the elderly. Despite their demographic differences, these attacks seemed eerily familiar, and I was floored by how common these incidents had become. I wanted to reach out to these families, send them a letter, or simply tell them I understand.

I think that's the mission I had in mind as I stood before the grand oak doors of the hearing room. To say I was intimidated is an understatement. The thought of telling my story to Connecticut legislators, being filmed on camera, and being viewed by an overflow room of environmental activists made my stomach drop. *What if they hate me and think that I'm seeking retribution against animals? What if I'm booed out of the room?* Nonetheless, I pushed open the doors wide, and I stepped through the threshold.

The hearing room was packed with people, and every seat was filled, making the room hot and stuffy. Those who couldn't find a seat stood, clinging to the opportunity to be in the room where the important decisions would be made. Activists who had come to speak about other issues packed into the room wearing stickers to signify their cause: whale reproductive rights, banning plastic initiative, and many more.

In the center of the room was a large, oval wooden desk with leather seats and microphones. The chairmen sat in the front of the room, each with an official plaque marking their name and filling the air with their authority. They would ultimately be the people to decide the fate of my cause.

State Representative Terrie Wood beckoned me in, wearing a distinguished pantsuit and a warm smile on her face. I had met with her before and emailed her many times to work out the logistics of legislation that could prevent further dog attacks like the one I had encountered. At the time, Connecticut had some of the weakest laws against dog attacks and to protect victims of any such violence. I advocated for a non-breed specific law that would label dogs "dangerous," and thus create a whole set of new policies for dangerous dogs to be rehabilitated and to have insurance compensate victims. I hoped that the points of the bill would prevent owners from being negligent (like letting dangerous dogs off leash in public spaces) and to take care of their dogs before they could harm anyone.

That's exactly what I planned to get across in my testimony. I had written countless drafts of it before, marked up pages with notes and crumpled up papers, and practiced my speech for hours. I infused my story and what I had suffered through in the testimony, and I hoped that people would understand that I was not looking for revenge--I was trying to find a silver lining.

Representative Wood helped me plan to take action. She dedicated many hours to my cause and sympathized with every word I said. Each time I told her my story, I could see the hurt and pain in her eyes, as she was deeply moved and motivated to help me create the change I wanted to see.

I was amazed that day Representative Wood took me and my parents around for a tour of the gorgeous capitol. She introduced us to many politicians who were impressed that I was there to testify at such a young age. They were intrigued that I was so willing to talk about what happened to me and able to stand my ground in front of adults to present my ideas.

My only fear was that people wouldn't take a seventeen year old seriously.

I watched other speakers come up to the microphone and pitch their legislation. Through the inflections and tone of each speaker's voice, it was obvious that each was deeply passionate about not only their bill, but about the cause behind it. Like me, they waited all day in a sticky meeting room to speak for a mere twenty minutes. They made every second count. That day, I learned how the people are the cogs of the machine that allow the government to run smoothly, it was beautiful to see activists in action, and I was honored to consider myself one of them.

When my bill was finally called, I stood up tall and walked with the straightest, most confident posture I could muster. As I stepped up to the pedestal that day, my youth melted away. I was a person, a citizen like any other. A girl who had undergone so much, but still dared to speak about it. I opened my mouth, and began to speak. My thoughts echoed off of each of the walls, and I felt the weight of over a hundred eyes settle on me. Except for my voice, the room was silent.

After finishing my testimony and answering spontaneous questions by the chair-people, we finally left the hearing room after several hours. My dad's eyes watered with tears. My mom was glowing with pride. Maybe it was because I had stood my ground when fired questions and responded like an adult. Maybe it was because I had finally come to the crux of what I had been working on for weeks. Maybe it was because they saw their daughter not bloodied and broken, but determined to make a difference.

March 20th, 2020

It's hard to think about your own problems and issues and even compare them with the impending doom of the rest of the world. Someone always has it worse. The year 2020 will be one remembered in world history, known for its chaos and tragedy. The thing I will remember the most from quarantine during the COVID-19 pandemic is not the illness itself: I remember the quiet. I think that whoever is reading this will remember some form of silence at this time. For me, it was a catastrophic break in the monotony and routine that had become normalized in my junior year of high school. Before the pandemic, I could barely find time to spend with my family, take a breath, or do my favorite things such as bake.

The quarantine provided something that I had long ago forgotten existed: time. Cut off from the bustling world that had once kept me afloat, I was left solely to exist in the bubble of my home, finding entertainment from myself rather than being surrounded by the noise of others.

I was devastated by this at first. My life-line of friends and school had been stripped from me. The fate of my beloved tennis season was uncertain, and I hoped more than anything for it to go on after the heartbreak of the dog attack and losing the end of my season last year. I was uncertain about my future, with college applications looming so soon. Everything seemed to be in disarray. Yet I had time, something that I had always wished for in the middle of studying for a major test, or longing for some rest from long school days.

The chaos on a global scale was even more intimidating: the hundreds of thousands of innocent lives that were expected to be lost, the fear for the health of people I loved the most, and the pure unknown of this pandemic. It was an overwhelming time for the whole world, and I never would have expected to have gained so much clarity into my own trauma at this unstable moment of time. It was hard to remember anything else mattered or existed when the only issue blaring on the news was COVID-19, day after day, night after night.

Yet at the same time, my own thoughts burned fiercer and more clearly than ever in my mind. I realized it was hard to forget my own thoughts when I was the only one around. I was left alone in the silence of my own thoughts--and these thoughts became very loud. The silence, interestingly enough, is what inspired me to write.

May 11th, 2020

One year later. My family joked that we should keep me locked inside and wrapped in bubble wrap to prevent anything bad from happening to me on this day. This day will always be a tough one. I had imagined that after a year, everything would come full circle and be tied up neatly in a bow. After one year, I would not be afraid of dogs any more, and my trauma would be healed in a perfect cycle. That would be too easy.

That day, I was home alone and I disobeyed my parents' joking orders: I took the car, and I went out. I could feel an intangible force pulling me, and I instinctively knew where I was driving, and I could not stop myself from going there. I had passed the Cove Beach several times before on my way home from fitness at Chelsea Piers. I'd sometimes choose to go out the back entrance, just so I could pass by the tennis courts where the incident occurred. As I drove by, I would turn my head slightly to the right and watch as the courts flew rapidly by the window. Three seconds and they were gone.

When I drove to the Cove Beach on May 11th, I could not control myself, so I slipped into the parking lot. There was no parking attendant, and I drove right in. But I hesitated before I turned to the right towards the parking spots in front of the basketball and tennis courts. There was still an invisible force holding me back--some protective instinct. Instead, I turned to the left and parked far away from the courts but where they were still in sight.

I squinted like I was searching for something, some monumental change, landmark, or sign that would indicate something had happened here, some marker that a girl had endured some of the most brutal moments of her life here. But there was nothing. Kids played pickup games of basketball, families strolled through the park, and players hit on the tennis courts as if nothing had happened. Life went on as normal.

Disappointed, I pulled out of the parking lot, and I drove home. No one knew I went there that day. That was my little secret.

May 13th, 2020

Like many others during the COVID-19 pandemic, my family and I sought relief from the confines of quarantine in nature. Never had as many people exercised, spent time outside, or taken walks as during these months.

Taking walks outside brought a rush of freedom and tranquility. It also provided ample time to bond with family members. My mom and I went on a special route which we dubbed "the loop" that wrapped around our house and Woodland Park.

By this time, I was far more confident taking walks outside the predictable comfort of my home. Before, I had always approached walks with the dread of possibly bumping into a dog out for a walk or a pet running from its backyard. But for some reason, these fears had melted away. I felt invincible, safe.

Maybe that's why when my mom and I were about halfway around the loop I suggested we walk through the woods. It was a shortcut to get back to the house, and at that point my legs were already aching and my mom was dripping with sweat. To many, walking through the woods may seem like a mundane, everyday task, but for me, this was a turning point in my healing process.

Despite living next door and practically being immersed in the woods, I had convinced myself I would never go into Woodland Park again. The woods were overflowing with hikers who brought along dogs running rampantly off-leash. This was a sight I witnessed often from the kitchen nook in my house--one time during breakfast, my dad and I jokingly counted how many dogs ran past us off-leash. In the span of twenty minutes, we counted seven. I had not stepped foot inside the park since the day before the dog attack, ironically: it was the last day that I was truly comfortable in nature.

Nonetheless, that day on the walk with my mom, I randomly had the urge to conquer the woods. The canopy of trees lured me in, not only as a short-cut to my house, but as an opportunity to conquer this fear that I was harboring. My mom stood stunned as I remarked my wish to her. I watched her thumb her keys and the pepper spray attached (which she always took walking with me) and hesitate a moment. Then she shrugged and nodded towards the woods: "Well, if you really want to. Let's do it."

I entered the threshold of the woods, never questioning my choice. The lighting instantly became darker as the thick foliage filtered out the sunlight. The woods were quiet save for the tweeting of a few stray birds, and it was empty of all human life. We wove our way through the paths, my mom likely more concerned about ticks, as always, than my worry about encountering any dogs. I jokingly told myself *if I took on a pit bull before, I can do it again.*

I heard a playful barking in the distance, and my throat tightened slightly, urging me to quicken my pace. But I didn't. My mom was next to me, I was close to home, and I was fine. *I'm fine,* I reassured myself. Instead, I focused on my soft footprints in the mud, the rustling of leaves, and the smell of dew on the trees.

I had forgotten how peaceful it could be to take a walk in the woods. When we finally reached the end of our journey, I was almost disappointed to leave the tranquility.

I don't think that my story would be authentic and truthful if I made this perfect arc where I was "cured" at the ending and could tie up all the loose ends in a neat bow. This is because a few days later, we went out on a walk again. We went around the same loop but this time took the long way instead of cutting through the woods. When we turned the corner onto the street adjacent to mine, I spotted a man several yards away. He was still barely a speck in the distance, but I could tell it was the same man I had seen many months before. I had seen him that day coming home from the physical therapist when I hid helplessly in the car, stunned by the irony. Here again, after I had just recently conquered the woods, was the man and his white pit bull. He only lived a street over, but I had always hoped I would never have to see his dog again. There was a striking resemblance between this dog and the one that attacked me. They had the same muscular legs, white fur and beady red eyes. This dog strained against his leash, wanting to rip away.

I turned to look at my mom, and her eyes embraced me with a knowing glance. She knew I was afraid. I didn't want to be, but I was scared. Looking at that dog I was brought back to that terrifying day and that horrifying struggle. He was still a ways away, but I was not going to take my chances, I was going to protect myself like I wish I could have on the day of the attack. So I ran.

As my breath was thrown around in my throat and fought its way in and out, my stomach cramped from the sudden burst of energy. At that moment, I thought I had failed. I couldn't stand my ground and confront the very image of my fear head-on. I had come so far with my optimism, with embracing my scars, and with taking on the woods. Reflecting back on this, I now know something I didn't understand at the time: healing from trauma is not a linear path. It is not a simple start to finish that ends in zero fear and invincibility. Healing is a cycle, a sine curve if you will, a continual system of failures and triumphs.

There is no timeline for when I will be able to say "I'm not afraid of dogs anymore" or "I don't feel self-conscious in my skin." There is no magical button to press to level-up in the game of mental healing. I wish I could have faced the dog and not ran away, but I know that I was not ready. I'm hopeful I will be someday.

June 2020

It was rather difficult to play tennis throughout the months of quarantine and into the summer. Early on, the town began to notice citizens' sudden pique in interest to play tennis (or rather, to find any way to leave their homes) and all of the courts were shut down in town. My amateur tennis career ground to a halt. Not only had I lost my entire high school season with my team due to COVID-19, but I had lost the ability to play the game I love, even on my own.

Amidst this fog of uncertainty, our guardian angel took shape: the Franks, family friends through my dad's work at Wee Burn, were kind enough to offer us their court to play on at their house. As a result of this stroke of luck, my sister and I had never been so energized to play than when we were starved of tennis these months. Also, my mom was excited to play more tennis than she had in a while, mostly because I dragged her to the court when I needed a hitting partner.

As a family, we went countless times to the Franks' tennis court during the pandemic. We played games, filmed a recruitment video, and refined our strokes as best we could. I annoyed my family by vainly shooting at the basketball hoop with my tennis balls. I practiced tennis trick shots that were only impressive to myself. Some of the happiest moments of the early pandemic took place on that single court.

The lush backyard with the tall trees and thick ever-growing foliage wrapped us in a cocoon and allowed us to temporarily forget the worries of the world. At that point, driving to the Franks' house and playing tennis on their court had become an escape from the monotony of our house and quarantine life. It was an adventure.

I watched the seasons change as the weeks passed on the tennis court: the trees filled in to become robust and provide a shield from the sun, the flowers broke out into bloom, and the wildlife sang in harmony. That green tennis court blended into the nature surrounding it, and it seemed perfectly nestled into the backyard, invisible to the rest of the world. I always felt safe. But there was one problem: the Franks' next door neighbors owned not one, but five dogs.

It started as a sound in the distance-- a barking noise that grew into a cacophony of howling dogs conversing with one another. The first time I heard this, I spun around in a circle, expecting an attack from any side and preparing for an enemy invasion. I could not see anything through the thick foliage; however, I saw a flash of white streak across the neighbor's lawn.

Behind the green, chain-link fence, I watched a fluffy white dog prance towards the border between the two properties. Sensing our movements, the dog glared in our direction and barked at us as though we were trespassers, issuing an order for us intruders to leave. We tried to continue playing, but his desperate pleas grew louder and louder, attracting attention from other dogs. I watched as another, smaller spotted dog appeared on the other side of the fence, shrouded by the larger dog and bearing a high-pitched chirpy bark.

My stomach dropped as I watched another dog, a large black one this time, lope over to his friend and proceed to bark in unison. This dog tried to traverse the divide between the Franks' house and their neighbors, butting its head forward and moving closer to the fence. These dogs stood lined up in a row, an army staring down its enemy. They stood grounded and unmoving. Their presence shook my body and sent shivers up my spine. I fumbled with the racket in my hand, hesitating from playing.

I instinctively looked for an escape route. I urgently checked each of the two gates to ensure they were secure. The smaller one was latched tightly, but the other was perplexing. I stared in disbelief at this metal gate, pulling, twisting, and sliding the latch to try to make it click into place. But to no avail, the lock was broken. The gate remained propped open.

Again, it was only the smallest sliver, a mere six inches, much like the gap from the Cove Beach that fateful day. I knew that six inches was enough to be invaded. Six inches of empty space between the fence was a wide abyss in my eyes. Spotting a worn, yellow rope attached to one side of the gate, I tied a hurried knot to connect both sides of the fence. The rope was fraying, and I willed it to hold.

All I wanted to do in the moment was dart off the court and plunge into the safety of our car, but my mom insisted that we keep playing. Her words stopped me like a leash holding me firm on the court.

I tiptoed back to the baseline and bounced on my toes in anticipation. My feet struck the pavement rhythmically as my blood beat through my body. The dogs remained, watching intently as I struck each ball and ran to recover. Slowly, they faded out of focus and were no longer intimidating creatures, but rather spectators clinging to their seats as they watched us play. They filtered away from the tennis court and back to their own backyard. When I turned around, they were gone.

I had continued to play tennis at the Franks' house about every other day, and the dogs, or our "friends," as we called them, visited like clockwork. Nonetheless, each day I stayed to play, I became stronger and more confident until I could even play on the side closest to the dogs.

After conquering my fear of the dogs, there was one day that stood out to me. We came to play early in the morning, and a windstorm had hit the night before. The court was littered with small leaves and sticks that had flown through the air.

The court had a different atmosphere this time: it felt exposed, and there was little distinction between where the court ended and the backyard stopped. It felt as if there was no longer this wall of protection surrounding it. I was no longer corralled in, but open to the rest of the trees and nature.

That's around when my eyes fell upon the tennis court gate. My jaw dropped when I saw the flash of yellow rope unraveled and laying dirtied on the ground. Instead of tying the door shut, the gate stood unlatched and ajar.

At first I scrambled to pick up the rope and try to secure the court, as was my routine before playing tennis each time. However, the rope was frayed and could not hold the gate together anymore--the green metal creaked and rebelled as I mercilessly dragged the hinge to close the gap. It would not close.

I let go of the door and watched as it slid open, leaving that narrow gap. I questioned my instincts and the security blanket I had always relied on: I could not force this gate to shut. A realization struck me, and a smile pulled at the corners of my lips. I knew I did not need this arbitrary gate. So I turned around, bounced the yellow, fuzzy tennis ball, and I started to play.

July 25th, 2020

I'm sitting on my back porch, nestled with an ice cold glass of water in hand and comforted by the worn blue and white striped cushions, the same cushions that I sink into time and time again, feeling as though I am floating on a cloud. It's the same back porch where a year before it had been my refuge--where I watched my leg heal, practiced my stretches, and re-learned how to walk. It's the same rectangular backyard enclosed by the woods. There's still the soft songs of birds and the distant hum of traffic. Yet now, the air is humid and heavy, and I bask in the dog days of summer.

The branches of the trees are robust and vibrant, and my view into the woods is obscured. Yet I can hear the people who pass by: families escaping their homes, exercise junkies on their daily jog, and dog-walkers picking their way through the woods.

I forgot about the dogs. This realization wracks my whole body and sends a shiver up my spine--but a good kind of shiver. From the jangling of a collar to the barking for their owner, the presence of dogs is obvious, but somehow I don't seem to mind anymore.

I forgot about the gate. The picket fence is a stark white against the colorful leaves and flowers. Still, I forgot the very habit that I relied on the most: I didn't turn my head quickly to the left and right to check that the gates were latched shut. I think it's because it doesn't matter anymore-- I feel safe.

The closed gate is no longer my life-force holding me together, but an arbitrary symbol of safety that is truly impossible to reach. I remember the horror when I realized something: the fence was not even very high. Not even staked into the earth, I could knock the plastic fence down with a swift kick. I had sought comfort in this protection that was a mere 4 feet tall.

I am slapped with the reality that my sense of safety was an illusion, a figment of my imagination. White picket fences aren't fortresses in any way. If some dog, human, or fate itself wanted to jump over or squeeze between the white pickets, they could do it. But they'd have to get past me first.

Now, I've given up on the idea of the gate. With it tightly shut, I bottle everything inside me like a powder keg waiting to explode. If you keep a gate locked tightly, you protect yourself from the evils of the world, but also shut out anything good from coming in.

I don't think that this was an immediate notion, but more of something that had slowly been developing and budding inside me subconsciously. It was not this mystical wave that washed over me where I instantaneously decided I was no longer anxious anymore. Instead, these recognitions morphed gradually into acceptance.

My scars are a brownish-pink now. They faded over a long period of time from that intense dark purple, and you can glance over them if you're not looking directly at my leg. I run my fingers over them expecting them to be healed, but they are still raised like the ridges and grooves on a globe that indicate where the mountains are. The scars are my mountains, but they are flattening with the wear of time and with the work of my own hands. Whenever my mom or I massage my scars, I can feel that both of us push and rub as deep as possible, as though we have the power to move mountains. I like to think that we do.

As I lay flopped on the back porch on my favorite blue-cushioned couch, I type away on my laptop. It's overheating and making a loud fuzzy noise that almost sounds like an airplane taking off. On this digital machine, I have stored every thought that I could muster about the attack and aftermath that have molded me into who I am. Instead of indulging my story in a person, I have shared my secrets with a leather-bound notebook and now a computer screen. I feel freer, lighter.

I never knew that writing would be the cure that essentially healed me. I never thought that the words would fly from my heart to a page, take root, and blossom into peace.

My goal of this book has morphed over the process of creating it--through brainstorming, writing, editing, and publishing. But the common thread through it all, is that I want this journal to be more than just for myself. If my thoughts resonate with just one person, I have succeeded.

I now know trauma takes on a broad range of severities: it wears different clothes and varies for everyone. There is no switch to suddenly decide that you are “cured” or that it no longer bothers you. Trauma is an animal that will lurk and possess you, but also strengthen you. It doesn’t only make an interesting story, but it makes a complex and unique person. I now understand that healing is a holistic process: mind, body, and soul, healing doesn’t stop when the wounds close and the stitches are removed.

I have divulged some of my deepest inner thoughts, and I’m hoping that by the end of this journal, you’re taken back to your own May 11th. Rather than mourn what you have lost, you remind yourself of what you have gained. You think of every little facet of life that has resulted from these tiny instances that now makes up your fate. Instead of shutting out what happened, you leave the gate wide open.

Made in the USA
Middletown, DE
08 October 2020

21388547R00066